KU-423-467

£5

Dilemmas of the Desert War

The Libyan Campaign
1940–1942

DILEMMAS OF THE DESERT WAR

*The Libyan Campaign
1940–1942*

by

Michael Carver

SPELLMOUNT
Staplehurst

British Library Cataloguing in Publication Data:
A catalogue record for this book is available
from the British Library

Copyright © Michael Carver 1986, 2002

ISBN 1-86227-153-4

First published in the UK in 1986 by
B T Batsford Ltd

This edition published in 2002 by
Spellmount Limited
The Old Rectory
Staplehurst
Kent TN12 0AZ

Tel: 01580 893730
Fax: 01580 893731
E-mail: enquiries@spellmount.com
Website: www.spellmount.com

1 3 5 7 9 8 6 4 2

The right of Michael Carver to be identified
as the author of this work has been asserted by him
in accordance with the Copyright, Designs
and Patents Act 1988

All rights reserved. No part of this publication may be
reproduced, stored in a retrieval system or transmitted in
any form or by any means, electronic, mechanical,
photocopying, recording or otherwise,
without prior permission in writing from
Spellmount Limited, Publishers.

Printed in Great Britain by
T.J. International Limited, Padstow, Cornwall

CONTENTS

LIST OF PHOTOGRAPHS AND MAPS

Photographs

Maps   *page*

ACKNOWLEDGMENTS

The author wishes to thank Major Alastair Ritchie for granting access to the papers of his uncle, General Sir Neil Ritchie; the Keeper of the Public Record Office for permission to quote from War Diaries; and Christopher Dowling and Roderick Suddaby of the Imperial War Museum for their encouragement and help.

All the photographs are reproduced by courtesy of the Imperial War Museum, with the exception of nos. 14 and 16 from Ullstein Bilderdienst, Berlin; and no. 12 from Süddeutscher Verlag, Munich.

The maps were drawn by Elizabeth Dawlings.

PREFACE

Since my books on *El Alamein* and *Tobruk* were published in 1962 and 1964 respectively, much has been written about the campaign in North Africa from 1940 to 1943, some of it based on new material, but most of it repeating, in one form or another, judgements or myths which had been established by such works as John Connell's *Auchinleck*,[1] Corelli Barnett's *Desert Generals*[2] and Field Marshal Montgomery's *Memoirs*[3]. Most of the senior commanders and staff officers of the time are now dead, and it was the death of General Sir Neil Ritchie[4] in December 1983 which inspired me to undertake a reassessment.

Both the pro-Auchinleck and the pro-Montgomery schools have been very critical of Ritchie's command of Eighth Army from 26 November 1941 to 25 June 1942. In the face of serious criticism, which he regarded as grossly unfair, he maintained a dignified silence and would not allow anybody access to his papers or to engage in public rebuttal of his critics on his behalf. He left his papers to his nephew, Major Alastair Ritchie, who deposited them at the Imperial War Museum, London, where, with his permission, I have had access to them.

They reveal how deeply General Ritchie resented the fact that Auchinleck had allowed Connell to publish an account so very, and in Ritchie's view unfairly, critical of him. He had been sent a proof copy of that part of the book which dealt with his period in command of Eighth Army, with a letter explaining that it had been approved by Auchinleck. Ritchie was unable to persuade Connell or the publishers to change more than a few details, and considered taking legal action. In a letter to the wife of the author of another book on Auchinleck, who was one of the latter's worshippers, he explained why:

To do this would have created a lot of ill-feeling and doubtless involve me in my version of how things in the Western Desert developed and which must have been critical of, and hurt others, including Auchinleck himself. This I had determined I would not do, but would continue to shoulder the blame myself.

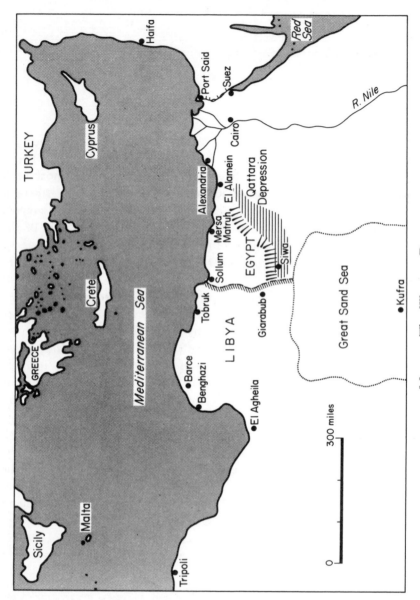

Map 1   The Western Desert

I simply could not believe that Auchinleck could have allowed the book to be written with apparently his approval, in view of our close relationship in the past.

So the following year [1960], when I was in Britain, I got Auchinleck to lunch with me and told him my feelings about the book. To my utter amazement, his only reaction was that the views were the author's and not his. Indeed he made it quite clear that he would do nothing to support or help me. He intended to let the blame for all that had gone wrong in the desert rest on my shoulders. He would not do anything to alter the inaccuracies contained in the book about me which, if you have read it, was written very much biased against me. This he could easily have done at the time.

From that day, my feelings for him completely changed. He did to me what I consider a dishonourable and disloyal thing.[5]

Ritchie felt that he had throughout been steadfastly loyal to the superior who, he considered (agreeing with many of his critics), should not have appointed him to command Eighth Army in the first place. He thought that, when Auchinleck dismissed Cunningham[6] in November 1941, he should have assumed command of Eighth Army himself, until a new commander could be sent from England, as both the Prime Minister and the CIGS, Dill,[7] suggested. Ritchie protested at the time, but loyally accepted when Auchinleck insisted. Sensitive to this 'special relationship', he was always at pains to keep his superior fully informed of his thoughts and of events, and to pay great attention to his advice. As a result, he was criticized by his subordinates, notably his two corps commanders, Gott[8] and Norrie,[9] as merely being the mouthpiece of the Commander-in-Chief, who, back in Cairo, was not only out of touch, but under the sinister influence of Brigadier (later Major-General) Dorman-Smith, who, on 18 May 1942, was appointed to Ritchie's former post of Deputy Chief of the General Staff at GHQ. When the latter was dismissed along with Auchinleck in August 1942, an event from which his army career never recovered, he laid all the blame at Ritchie's door, and Ritchie believed that Dorman-Smith was to blame for unsatisfactory advice from GHQ and for causing differences between himself and Auchinleck. There is no doubt that Dorman-Smith was the principal source of the highly critical tone both of Connell's book and of Barnett's. After his own dismissal, Ritchie never uttered a word of criticism of Auchinleck, nor of any of his subordinates, two of whom, Norrie and Messervy,[10] had no such inhibitions.

In this book I have attempted to take a fresh look at the campaign, dealing with the major issues, but concentrating on the period which has invited most of the criticism: from 27 May 1942, when Rommel launched his attack on Eighth Army at Gazala, to 25 June, when Auchinleck dismissed Ritchie and assumed personal command himself. I have examined this period in great detail, for, unless one does so, it is not possible to arrive at an objective view of just what happened and why; and who was then to blame for the disastrous defeat which brought Eighth Army back to El Alamein.

I have followed the story from its beginning in May 1940 up to the end of the Battle of El Alamein, but have not attempted to comment on Montgomery's progress after that, westward along the coast of North Africa until Eighth Army joined hands with the First in Tunisia.

On some pages, in describing the action or commenting on it, I have used extracts from my book *Tobruk*. They are annotated, and the exact reference given in the Notes.

O N E

VICTORY OVER
THE ITALIANS

The operations in which the British army was engaged from May 1940 until
the end of 1942, in the desert backing the southern shore of the Mediterranean westward from the Nile valley to the cultivated area of Libya round
Tripoli, were unlike any other in which they, or any other army, had
previously been engaged. Tanks, in the First World War, had been slow,
cumbersome beasts, designed to support deliberate infantry attacks.
Although more mobile ones had seen action in 1918, they had not been
radically different. Tanks had practically never fought other tanks. Experience with tanks in that war was of no help, except in operations which
involved the close support of infantry in the attack. Nobody, senior or junior
whatever their arm of the service, had any experience of highly mobile
operations, ranging over wide areas, in which tanks fought each other. In
default of experience, the army had to rely either on theory or, as most
commanders did, on what they regarded as pragmatic common sense or even
happy-go-lucky intuition. Such theory as there was had been developed
within the Royal Tank Corps. It differentiated clearly between tanks
employed for the direct support of infantry and those which would be used
in independent mobile operations, ranging far and wide behind the enemy
lines. The latter school of thought, following the precepts of those apostles
of mobility, Fuller and Liddell Hart, tended to gloss over the problems of
how the tanks got there and what was liable to happen on the way. In
addition to these rôles, the official view envisaged the function of 'mechan-
ized cavalry' as providing a covering force which would enable a commander
to discover the enemy's dispositions and strength, and probe his intention,
before he committed his main force. Within the school which envisaged an
armoured force as operating independently, there were differences of opinion
between those who favoured a balanced force of arms, their vehicles all being
tracked and armoured, and those who envisaged a force consisting almost
exclusively of tanks. Liddell Hart was of the first: Major-General Hobart,[1]
who in 1938 and 1939 formed and trained the formation known originally as

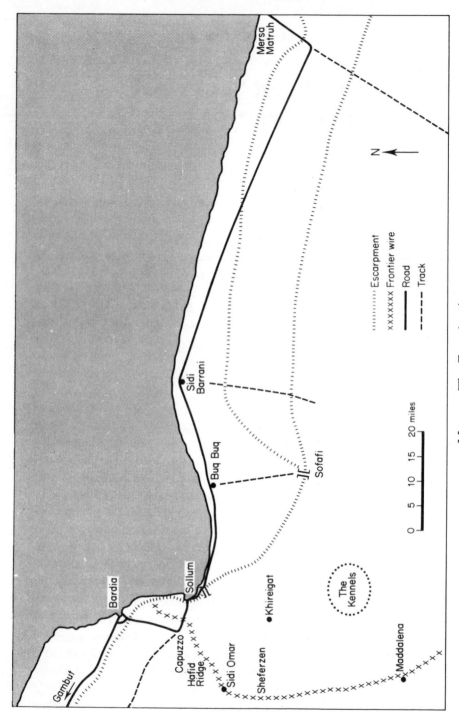

Map 2   The Frontier Area

Mobile Division (Egypt) and later as 7th Armoured Division, was of the second. He was a man of great energy and determination, who impressed his personality and views very firmly on his division. They were not approved of by his superior, General Maitland Wilson,[2] on whose recommendation he was sacked by Wavell[3] in November 1939.

Whatever theories anybody may have believed in, the hard facts were that the resources to carry out any of them did not exist. When Italy declared war in May 1940, the force available to Wavell amounted to no more than 40,000 men. To face Marshal Balbo's Tenth Italian Army of 70,000 men in Libya, the only force immediately available was Creagh's[4] 7th Armoured Division with only one of its two armoured brigades, and that had only two regiments of tanks. One was equipped solely with light tanks, the other with a mixed collection of 'cruisers', some of which were still awaiting delivery of their guns.

The performance of the German armoured divisions in Poland in 1939 and France in 1940 and the dramatic success of O'Connor's[5] offensive against the Italians, starting at Sidi Barrani on 8 December 1940 and reaching a triumphant conclusion at Beda Fomm, south of Benghazi, on 7 February 1941, appeared strongly to reinforce the school who believed that mobility alone, provided by tanks as the principal arm, could bring victory. The pattern of O'Connor's campaign had reinforced pre-war concepts. The one regiment of heavy, slow infantry support, or 'I', tanks – the Matildas of Colonel Jerram's 7th Royal Tanks – had supported in succession the attacks of 4th Indian Division at Sidi Barrani and 6th Australian Division at Bardia and Tobruk to great effect, while 7th Armoured Division's lightly armoured cruiser and light tanks had outflanked and surrounded the static Italian garrisons, preceded and covered by the ancient armoured cars of the 11th Hussars. At the cost of less than 2000 casualties of whom 500 were killed, O'Connor's army, which at Beda Fomm consisted only of 22 cruiser and 45 light tanks, 24 field guns, one armoured car regiment and one motor infantry battalion, had totally defeated an army of ten divisions, capturing 130,000 prisoners, 380 tanks and 845 guns.

Nothing in that campaign caused those concerned with armoured warfare to doubt the validity of their training or of the concepts of how tanks should be employed. The fact that the Italian army had never challenged British tanks in mobile operations, and, with the exception of its artillery, had never fought hard, for the most part sitting immobile and inactive behind its fixed defences, obscured the fact that, unlike 7th Royal Tanks' Matildas, the tanks of 7th Armoured Division had hardly had to fight at all, except for the few which reached Beda Fomm. Their principal problem had been logistic: to keep their tanks supplied with fuel and mechanically fit. Nor had there been any great need for the co-operation of tanks, infantry and artillery within the division. The experience of the campaign encouraged two tendencies which were to have a pernicious influence on subsequent operations. The first arose from the threat of air attack. There was no possibility of concealment from the air in the desert. Although, at all important times, the RAF, in spite of its exiguous stock of antiquated aircraft, had dominated the Italian Regia Aeronautica, enemy air attacks and reconnaissance could not be eliminated. A very wide dispersion of units, and of individual vehicles within them, was adopted as a measure both of protection and of concealment of intention. This dispersion became a hallmark of 'desert-worthiness'. It persisted when the need for it did not exist, and encouraged a tactical dispersion which militated against effective concentration of firepower on the battlefield.

The second tendency arose from the need to conserve resources, particularly of tanks. The mileage which tanks could clock up before tracks or engine needed repair or replacement was limited. Distances were great and wear-and-tear on both in the desert was high. In periods between major operations, 'columns', composed of a company of motorized infantry and either a troop or a battery of field artillery, were employed to harass the enemy, to support the armoured cars in keeping contact with him, and to keep him from divining our intentions. This was the origin of 'Jock' columns, called after Jock Campbell,[6] the gallant commander of 4th Regiment Royal Horse Artillery. These columns served well the purpose for which they were originally designed, and those who fought in them greatly preferred the excitement, tinged with not too great a degree of danger, which their operation involved, to sitting doing nothing or to more pedestrian artillery rôles. Unfortunately their success in O'Connor's campaign, culminating in the successful blocking of the road south of Beda Fomm, led to an exaggerated idea of the effect their action would have on a more resolute and better-trained enemy; and discouraged the development of a closer co-operation between the tanks of the armoured division, concentrated in its armoured brigades, and its artillery and infantry, grouped together in the Support Group. In any case, the offensive strength of the latter was very limited. The artillery consisted only of one field artillery regiment and one combined anti-tank and anti-aircraft regiment; and the infantry of two 'motor' battalions with an infantry strength (excluding drivers) of only some 400 men each, and no armoured vehicle, other than the Bren Gun carrier, in which to advance towards the enemy.

The two controversial strategic decisions of the campaign came respectively at the beginning and the end. The first was Wavell's decision to replace

4th Indian Division by 6th Australian immediately after the battle of Sidi Barrani: the second, not to permit an advance to Tripoli after Beda Fomm. To O'Connor, at the time, both appeared to be failures to exploit the favourable opportunities offered by his victory; but Wavell's judgement was probably correct on both occasions.

The reason for the first decision was that 4th Indian Division, both on account of its character and training and also for administrative reasons, was more suitable than the inexperienced Australian for employment in Platt's[7] force attacking the Italians in Abyssinia. O'Connor's operation had been planned by Wavell as a limited one: to destroy the Italian army which had crossed the Libyan frontier in September, and it was only expected to last five days. It would ensure that Wavell's main base in Egypt was made secure, while he dealt with the Italians in East Africa. Although the delay imposed by the change-over was frustrating to O'Connor, it is unlikely that it made any significant difference to the campaign. The principal determining factor in the speed with which the subsequent advance could be conducted was logistic, and the key to that was the availability of motor transport. It is just possible, however, that the delay of about ten days could have been critical. If victory at Beda Fomm had been achieved ten days earlier, and if then Wavell had permitted an advance to Tripoli, O'Connor might have been able to get a light force there before the first ship bringing Rommel's 5th Light Panzer Division had arrived, which it did on 12 February 1941.

However, the reasons which prompted Wavell to refuse permission for such an advance would also have prevailed then. They were that priority had been given to the despatch of a force to Greece. That had been the case since November. Churchill and the Chiefs of Staff had been anxious that Wavell should not get committed too far west in Libya, and on 10 January Churchill had signalled: 'Nothing must hamper capture of Tobruk but thereafter all operations in Libya are subordinated to aiding Greece.[8]

The disastrous strategic decision to despatch a force to Greece is directly relevant to our story but will not be described here. At the time, and for long after, it was felt that Wavell had been pushed into it by pressure, not only from Eden and the CIGS, Dill, on their visit, but by Churchill and the Chiefs of Staff. But it is now clear that by 6 March pressure from London had eased. On that day Churchill had sent a signal to Eden, returned from Athens to Cairo, in which, reflecting the sober views of the Chiefs of Staff, he said:

We must be careful not to urge Greece against her better judgement into a hopeless resistance alone when we have only handfuls of troops which can reach the scene in time. Grave Imperial issues are raised by committing New Zealand and Australian troops to an enterprise which, as you say, has become even more hazardous. We are bound to lay before the Dominions Governments your and Chiefs of Staff appreciation. Cannot forecast their assent to operation. We do not see any reasons for expecting success, except that of course we attach great weight to opinions of Dill and Wavell.[9]

But by that time Wavell and his colleagues were in favour, and their reply next day[10] was the decisive factor in the decision to send the force, largely New Zealand and Australian, with such unfortunate consequences.

O'Connor was deeply disappointed, and, while he was a prisoner of war and for long after, brooded on whether or not a golden opportunity was missed, which would have altered the whole course of the North African campaign and, incidentally, prevented him from having had to endure captivity. But his Brigadier General Staff, Harding,[11] believed that, even if he had been allowed to send light forces on towards Tripoli, they would not have been able to stay there. The lack of air, naval and logistic support would have precluded it, and the Italians alone could have produced greatly superior force there.

T W O

BACK TO *BATTLEAXE*

Intelligence told Wavell a fortnight after Beda Fomm that German troops had reached Tripoli; however, he felt confident at first that he could leave the defence of Cyrenaica to 'only a small armoured force and one partly trained Australian division'[1] the commanders of which, from top to bottom, were completely inexperienced. Wilson had at first replaced O'Connor, but had then been put in command of the expedition to Greece and had handed over to Neame,[2] who had been commanding the troops in Palestine. Wavell thought that the enemy would not be in a position to take the offensive until May at the earliest, and his orders to Neame were that, if he were attacked, he was to fight a delaying action between his forward position at Mersa Brega and Benghazi, a distance of 150 miles. He was not to hesitate to give ground, even evacuating Benghazi if necessary, but holding on to the high ground east of Benghazi for as long as possible. He could expect no reinforcement until May, and must therefore conserve his armoured troops as much as possible.[3]

Neame's armoured troops were not an impressive collection. As 2nd Armoured Division arrived in the desert to relieve the 7th in January, its commander, Major-General J. C. Tilly, had died and been replaced by another Royal Tank Corps officer, Major-General M. D. Gambier-Parry, who had been head of the miliary mission to Greece and had no recent experience of command. Its 3rd Armoured Brigade consisted of one under-strength regiment of light tanks, one equipped with the Italian M13 medium tanks captured at Beda Fomm, and one of cruisers which did not arrive in the forward area until the second half of March, and, having travelled on its tracks all the way from El Adem, was in a poor mechanical state.

On 20 March the division took over responsibility for the whole forward area from Morshead's[4] 9th Australian Division, whose two brigades, totalling only five battalions, were withdrawn to the high ground to the north, the Jebel or 'Bulge' of Cyrenaica. For logistic reasons its third brigade had to remain in Tobruk. Neame was distinctly unhappy at his lack of troops and of transport, which made them dependent on static supply depots, and at the state of his mobile forces; and Wavell himself had begun to have qualms

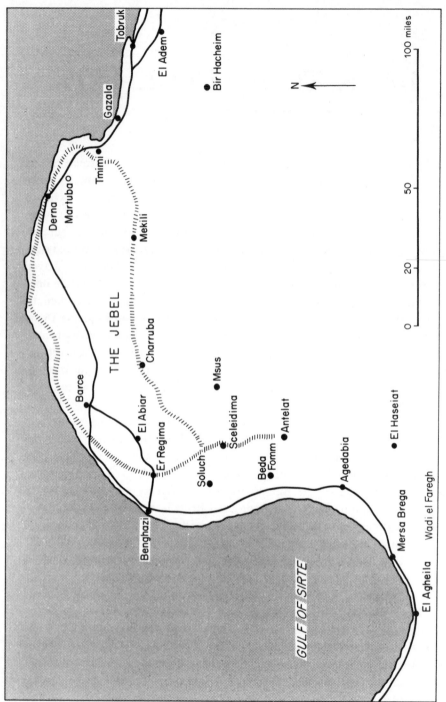

Map 3 Cyrenaica

by 23 March, when he stated in a signal to Churchill: 'I have to admit to have taken a considerable risk in Cyrenaica after capture of Benghazi, in order to provide maximum support to Greece.'[5] That risk became evident when, on 24 March, a German reconnaisance unit drove a patrol of British armoured cars out of El Agheila. A week passed before any further move was made. On 31 March Streich's 5th Light Panzer Division, with about 70 light and 80 medium tanks, attacked 2nd Armoured Division's Support Group's positions astride the coast road at Mersa Brega. Its commander, Latham,[6] asked for help from Rimington's 3rd Armoured Brigade, which was five miles away to the north-east, but Gambier-Parry ruled that there was not enough time before dark for it to be effective. That night Latham withdrew to Agedabia, Rimington conforming. Little happened next day. On 2 April Neame told Gambier-Parry that the armoured brigade should not be committed without permission; that it would have to rely on supply from the depot at Msus, and that, although it should keep within supporting distance of the Support Group on the coast road, it must ensure that it could move east of the escarpment which ran parallel to the road some 30 miles east of it. Gambier-Parry protested that this would split his division and asked for freedom of action, even if it uncovered the coast road. Neame was about to agree when Wavell arrived at his headquarters and insisted that the Support Group should impose the maximum delay on an advance to Benghazi, and that, if withdrawal became necessary, the armoured brigade should move north to El Abiar and cover the left flank of the Australians – a reversal of his original orders, confirmed formally as recently as 26 March, which attached less importance to holding Benghazi. By this time Rimington's tank strength had fallen to 22 cruisers and 25 light tanks, and he was in difficulty over petrol supply.

Wavell's other decision was to summon O'Connor to fly up, accompanied by Brigadier Combe, until recently commanding officer of the 11th Hussars; his intention was that the former should replace Neame. From then on a combination of long delays in communications, resulting in misunderstandings and changes in orders, and a general breakdown of the logistical organization within 2nd Armoured Division, led to a collapse of any effective resistance. Rommel, in the face of protests from his Italian and German superiors, split his forces and sent them in all directions, only retaining some vestige of control by flying hither and thither in his Fieseler-Storch, narrowly avoiding capture by the British and nearly being shot down by his Italian allies. Rimington, Gambier-Parry, Neame, O'Connor and Combe were all captured. By good fortune Harding evaded it, and he and Morshead together, back at Tobruk on 7 April, organized a scratch defence from the troops available. Wavell flew up to see them on 8 April, and, having been assured by Harding that, provided that the Germans did not produce a mass of tanks and that the navy could maintain supplies by sea, Tobruk could be held, said: 'Well if you think you can hold it, you'd better,' and handed overall command to Major-General J. D. Lavarack, commander of 7th Australian Division, who had flown up with him. By 11 April Rommel had surrounded the old Italian defences, and the seven-and-a-half month siege of Tobruk began.

The blame for this disastrous reversal of fortunes must be attributed to failure to face realities at every level. The general state of the force, in terms of training, professional competence, logistic supply and serviceability of equipment, meant that it was no match for its opponent. In no sphere was this more so than in communications and the speed with which decisions were made, orders issued and communicated, and, when received, acted upon. Wavell must carry a large share of the blame; but one must remember that he had many other concerns at that time, notably preparations for the campaign in Greece. The Germans had shown that the sort of risks which could be accepted when fighting the Italians could not be taken with them; but Rommel had been lucky to have succeeded in an operation which, by any normal standard, would have been regarded as totally unsound: his own superiors certainly thought that – Halder called him 'this soldier gone stark mad' – and he was to find, when he came up against the tough Australians in Tobruk, that more conventional methods of warfare were needed.

Failure in Libya, Greece and Crete was followed by problems in Iraq and a five-week campaign against the Vichy French in Syria, but Churchill was not going to let matters rest in the desert. On 21 May, the day after the attack on Crete, he signalled to Wavell: 'Nothing in Syria must detract at this moment from winning the Battle of Crete or in the Western Desert.' A month before, at Churchill's instigation, the Defence Committee had decided to take the considerable risk of sending a convoy of five fast ships, carrying 300 tanks and a large number of Hurricane aircraft, through the Mediterranean. One ship was sunk and 238 tanks and 43 Hurricanes reached Alexandria on 12 May. Churchill pressed Wavell to make use of these 'Tiger Cubs', as he called them, as soon as possible to eject Rommel from the frontier and relieve Tobruk. Without waiting for them, Wavell had ordered Beresford-Peirse,[7] who had taken over command of Western Desert Force, to launch an attack to clear the Germans from Capuzzo and Halfaya Pass above Sollum, from which they had ejected Brigadier Gott's mobile force on 26 April; and, if successful in that, to exploit towards Tobruk as far as supply would allow and without endangering the force employed. All the troops involved in

Operation *Brevity* were under Gott's command, and it was not a large force. The principal element was 22nd Guards Brigade, supported by 24 Matildas of 4th Royal Tanks. It was to attack along the top of the escarpment, capture Halfaya and Capuzzo and exploit northwards. Below the escarpment, one battalion of 7th Support Group was to capture the foot of the pass and clear Sollum itself. On the outer flank, 7th Armoured Brigade, with only 29 cruiser tanks and three columns from the Support Group was to execute a wide flanking movement to Sidi Azeiz, 12 miles behind Capuzzo, and destroy any enemy they met. The operation was launched on 15 May and at first all went well; but Rommel reinforced the local commander, Colonel Herff, with a second battalion of tanks, and Gott, concerned at the vulnerability of the Guards Brigade, of which one battalion, in penetrating to Musaid, between Capuzzo and Sollum, had suffered heavy casualties, withdrew them to the position at the head of Halfaya Pass, which was the only gain from the operation; and that was lost on 26 May when Herff launched a surprise attack against it.

Wavell's motive in attempting what was undoubtedly a premature attempt to improve the situation on the frontier was to forestall the arrival of the 15th Panzer Division, which now joined 5th Light (later renamed 21st) in what was to be known as The Deutsches Afrika Korps (DAK). The division, commanded by Neumann-Silkow, relieved 5th Light on the frontier on 8 June and set about improving the defences, including the installation of 88mm anti-aircraft guns as anti-tank weapons. On 17 May Churchill, saying rather surprisingly that the results of *Brevity* 'seem to us satisfactory', had urged an early resumption of the attack ending his signal with the question: 'What are your dates for bringing Tiger Cubs into action?'[8] Wavell replied that it would not be before the end of the month 'and it would be better if they could be given more time'. Ten days later he told Dill that the earliest date for a move forward from Mersa Matruh would be 7 June and could be later. He gave a number of reasons why he thought that 'the measure of success which will attend this operation is in my opinion doubtful.'[9]

The depressing events in Wavell's command in the early months of 1941 in Libya, Greece and Crete did not seem to call for any reconsideration of concepts: indeed, they appeared to reinforce existing practice. In Libya, logistic difficulties and the lack of training of the recently arrived 2nd Armoured Division were blamed for its failure. In Greece and Crete, and to a lesser extent in Libya, the enemy air force appeared to be the principal threat. In Greece the army had seen little fighting, either before or during its withdrawal under constant air attack. In Crete it had been from lack of tanks and artillery of all kinds, rather than from any misuse of them, that the New

Zealand infantry had suffered. The undoubted confusion of the higher command tended to obscure tactical failure. Rommel's success in routing Neame's force and driving it back in confusion to Tobruk with a greatly inferior strength reinforced the view of those who believed that mobility alone could decide the day by producing 'ruin upon ruin, rout on rout, confusion worse confounded'.[10] Wavell, therefore had no particular reason to suggest to Beresford-Peirse that any radical change was needed in the tactical handling of the two divisions under his command, both of which had performed so brilliantly at Sidi Barrani six months before, and one of which, 4th Indian, he had himself commanded, earning further laurels at Keren in Abyssinia: the other was still under its original commander, Creagh.

The next offensive in the Western Desert, Operation *Battleaxe*, started on 15 June and employed two divisions: Messervy's 4th Indian had two brigades, 22nd Guards and 11th Indian, and Gatehouse's[11] 4th Armoured Brigade, which consisted of two regiments of Matildas, about 100 in all. In 7th Armoured Division, Creagh, besides his Support Group, had Russell's[12] 7th Armoured Brigade, which had only two regiments of tanks, one of newly arrived Crusaders and the other with a mixed collection of older cruisers. Beresford-Peirse's plan envisaged two phases. In the first, 4th Indian Division would destroy the enemy force in the area of Bardia-Sollum-Halfaya-Capuzzo, starting with the recapture of Halfaya, while 7th Armoured covered its left flank, 7th Armoured Brigade advancing by bounds to Hafid Ridge, six miles west of Capuzzo, and the Support Group forming a screen on its left. If 7th Armoured Brigade's advance attracted all the German tanks (the number of which was overestimated – it was actually about 100 in the forward area), Gatehouse's Matildas would move to join Creagh, and Messervy's principal attack towards Capuzzo would be delayed until the tank battle was over.

The battle did not work out as planned. The attack on Halfaya failed, 15 out of the 18 Matildas involved being lost to anti-tank fire and mines. Seventh Armoured Brigade came up against a powerful anti-tank defence, including four 88mms, on Hafid Ridge, which was later reinforced by a battalion of tanks. At 1030 hrs, no major tank battle having developed on the left, Messervy launched his attack in the centre, which was successful. By the end of the day the leading Matildas had penetrated beyond Capuzzo, although the infantry had not caught up with them, and they had to hang about, but Creagh's cruiser strength had been reduced to 48. Rommel's reaction was to order 15th Panzer Division to use its 8th Panzer Regiment to counter-attack Messervy's penetration next day, while 5th Light's 5th Panzer Regiment executed a wide movement round 7th Armoured Division's left flank into its rear. Messervy and Creagh countered these attacks but by the end of the day the latter's strength was down to 21 tanks and Messervy had not been able to release any of Gatehouse's Matildas to help him. However, with the Guards firmly ensconced at Capuzzo, he planned to do so on the 17th in the hope of thus defeating Rommel's armour. The latter, in spite of Neumann-Silkow's anxieties about a breakthrough towards Bardia, planned to use both Panzer Regiments in an encircling movement. On the inner flank 8th Panzer Regiment would cut behind Messervy from Hafid Ridge, while 5th Panzer outflanked Creagh, moving by Sidi Omar, both directed towards Halfaya. This attack started at dawn on the 17th and succeeded in its aim. Fifth Panzer had reached Sidi Suleiman by 0800 hrs, threatening to cut off Messervy and Gatehouse, whose tanks were short of ammunition. Creagh had difficulty in getting through to Beresford-Peirse, but at 0930 hrs succeeded, and told him that Russell was down to 22 cruiser and Gatehouse to 17 'I' tanks. Wavell had flown up to Beresford-Peirse's headquarters at Sidi Barrani, and flew on with him to Creagh, arriving at 1145 hrs. There he heard that Messervy, at 1100 hrs, had ordered 22nd Guards Brigade to withdraw. He immediately appreciated that it would be wrong to attempt to countermand it, ordered a complete withdrawal in order to reorganize, and returned to Cairo to face his own dismissal four days later. Beresford-Peirse and Creagh suffered the same fate. Casualties in human terms had been light – 122 killed, 588 wounded and 259 missing – but, of the 90 cruisers and 100 'I' tanks, 27 of the former and 64 of the latter were lost by enemy action or breakdowns which could not be recovered. From these figures, it is clear that most of the reduction of Russell's strength must have been from breakdowns, later repaired and recovered. German casualties were 93 killed, 350 wounded and 235 missing. Eighth Panzer Regiment started with about 100 tanks, of which half were light, and lost only 8, and 5th Panzer with 96, of which 39 were light, and lost only 4.

Recriminations and post-mortems followed. It was not immediately recognized that it was the German anti-tank guns, not their tanks, which had caused most of the tank casualties. Until *Battleaxe*, the Matilda had felt invulnerable on the battlefield, but the 88mm put paid to that. However their number was very limited. There were probably five at Halfaya, four on Hafid Ridge and four moving with 8th Panzer Regiment. Whether static or mobile, their high profile made them very vulnerable to artillery fire, but the tendency, in the infantry divisions, was to use that in immediate support of the infantry, and in the armoured, to employ it in a harassing rôle with the motor infantry of the Support Group. To those who took part in the battle, the lessons seemed to be that it was impossible to combine the action of the slow 'I' tanks with that of the cruisers of the armoured division, and that they should not therefore be counted as assets in the tank *v* tank balance; that the armoured division should not get involved in attacks against fixed defences in the area near the coast; and that Wavell was wrong in rejecting Beresford-Peirse's original plan for a wide sweep by 7th Armoured Division towards Tobruk, while 4th Indian tackled the frontier defences. These reactions to *Battleaxe* were to influence the plan for the next desert offensive, Operation *Crusader*.

THREE

CRUSADER

Auchinleck assumed command on 2 July and was immediately subjected to pressure from Churchill for a renewal of the offensive in the desert, to take advantage of the 'temporary German pre-occupation in their invasion of Russia';[1] the intention was to relieve Tobruk and establish airfields from which air cover could be provided for convoys sailing between Alexandria and Malta. This was the start of an argument about strategic priorities in the Middle East which was to continue throughout Auchinleck's tenure of command, aggravated by the German advance towards the Caucasus and Japanese entry into the war later in the year. To Auchinleck, the security of his base in the Nile valley, protecting the approaches to the vital oil sources of the Persian Gulf, was all-important. Exactly where it was defended from the west was not a vital matter. Malta was certainly of great importance to the campaign in the Western Desert, as from it air and submarine attacks on the enemy's supply line could be delivered; but it would be a reversal of priorities to embark prematurely, with doubtful prospects of success, on an offensive in the desert for the sake of Malta, or even of the relief of Tobruk, although maintenance of the besieged garrison was costing the navy dear.

Auchinleck's determination to avoid another *Battleaxe* and to give priority to securing his northern flank by finishing off the campaign against the French in Syria and 'securing Cyprus' was reinforced by what he believed to be the lessons of *Battleaxe*. The signal which he sent to Churchill only two days after assuming command, starting bluntly with the sentence, 'No further offensive Western Desert should be contemplated until base is secure', outlined the basic operational concept which was to determine the pattern of the next offensive in the desert. It continued:

It is quite clear to me that infantry divisions, however well trained and equipped, are no good for offensive operations in this terrain against enemy armoured forces. Infantry divisions are and will be needed to hold defended localities after enemy armoured forces have been neutralized and destroyed, but the main offensive must be carried out by armoured formations supported by motorized formations.[2]

This prudent attitude was anathema to Churchill, who replied:

Only by reconquering the lost airfields of eastern Cyrenaica can Fleet and Air Force

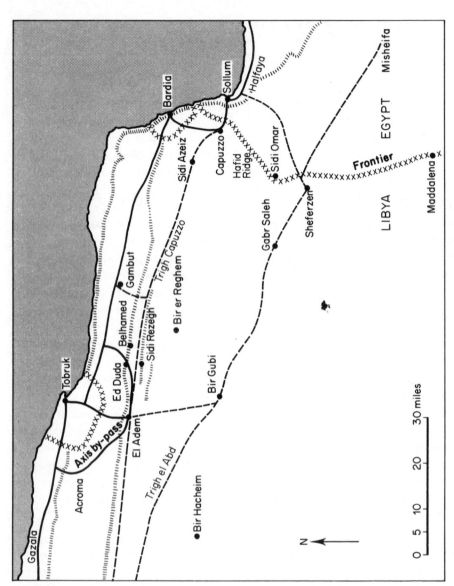

Map 4   The *Crusader* Battlefield

resume effective action against enemy's seaborne supplies. . . . It is difficult to see how your situation is going to be better after the middle of September than it is now and it may well be worsened. I have no doubt you will maturely but swiftly consider whole question . . .[3]

In spite of Admiral Cunningham's[4] keen desire to be rid of the burden of supplying Tobruk and both his and Air Marshal Tedder's[5] equally strong wish to base air forces further west to cover the route to Malta, both of them supported Auchinleck in his insistence that he needed sufficient strength in tanks before he could launch an offensive which had a reasonable prospect of success, not only of relieving Tobruk, but of securing the Bulge of Cyrenaica, thus obtaining airfields from which sailings to and from Malta could be given air cover. Auchinleck maintained that he needed three armoured divisions for this, although he would be prepared to undertake it with two. First Armoured Division was due to come from England, sailing round the Cape, but would not be complete and ready to take the field, giving him two armoured divisions, until January 1942. However, one of its brigades, the 22nd, would arrive in time to take part in operations from mid-November onwards. In spite of great pressure, exerted during a visit to England at the end of July, as well as in an almost continuous exchange of signals, Auchinleck could not be shifted from that date as the earliest on which he could undertake an offensive. Churchill's concern was not only that, while Auchinleck was building up his strength, Rommel and his Italian allies would be doing the same, but also that Rommel might have the strength to break into Tobruk before Auchinleck could raise the siege. The Australian government was pressing urgently for the relief of the predominantly Australian garrison, and in September Auchinleck was forced to carry out a relief by sea with the British 70th Division and the Polish Carpathian Brigade, an operation which placed a great strain on the navy.

The force in the desert was now to be raised to the status of an Army, to be numbered the Eighth, and 13th Corps joined by a newly (and hastily) created corps headquarters, the 30th. The question of who was to command them arose. The end of the campaign in Abyssinia made available the senior commanders involved in that, and two, who had been prominent in the virtually unopposed advance from Kenya to Addis Abbaba, were chosen: Cunningham for command of Eighth Army and Godwin-Austen for 13th Corps. Alan Cunningham, brother of Auchinleck's redoubtable naval colleague, was an artilleryman, who had commanded an anti-aircraft division of the Territorial Army from 1938 to 1940, and had then assumed command in East Africa, leading to his command of the force which invaded Italian East Africa from the south. Godwin-Austen, an infantryman, had been one of his subordinates, commanding the 12th East African Division, after having been in charge of the withdrawal from Somaliland.

While most of the infantry, supported by the 'I' tanks of 1st Army Tank Brigade, was to be in 13th Corps, the armoured and mobile forces were to be under 30th Corps, for the command of which Major-General Vyvyan Pope was flown out from England. Having commanded an infantry battalion in the First World War at the age of 25, he transferred after it to the Royal Tank Corps and had previous experience of the desert in an armoured car company. Having been Brigadier General Staff to Alan Brooke, when the latter's 2nd Corps was sent back to France through Cherbourg after Dunkirk, he had become Director of Armoured Fighting Vehicles at the War Office. Few senior officers could have been better qualified for the command. Unfortunately, on 6 October, he and his principal staff officers, one of whom was Russell, on their way to a conference with Cunningham, were killed when their aircraft crashed after take-off from Cairo. He was replaced by Major-General Willoughby Norrie, who, on his way out by sea in command of 1st Armoured Division, was flown up from South Africa. He was a cavalryman who had had some experience with tanks in the First World War.

Cunningham's plan, based on the principle which Auchinleck had enunciated in his first signal to Churchill, was for the 30th Corps to cross the Libyan frontier near Maddalena, 50 miles south of Sollum, and advance north-west towards Tobruk, joining hands with the garrison, which would make a sortie towards them. They would then roll up the Italian divisions to the west of them, while 13th Corps, having disposed of the Italian and German defences between Sollum and Sidi Omar, would advance west to join them. The difficulties and arguments began about the method by which this grand concept should be implemented. To understand them, we must consider the forces available to both sides.

Overall command of Italian and German troops in Libya was exercised by General Gariboldi (later General Bastico). As a result of a recent reorganization, Rommel commanded all troops east of the Cyrenaican Bulge, except for Gambara's 20th Italian Mobile Corps, consisting of Ariete Armoured and Trieste Mobile Divisions. His command was known as Panzergruppe Afrika (later Panzerarmee). Subordinate to him were Navarini's 21st Corps of four infantry divisions (Brescia, Pavia, Trento and Bologna), the Italian Savona division in the frontier defences, Crüwell's Afrika Korps and Böttcher's Artillery Command 104, a group of heavy artillery provided for the attack on Tobruk. The Afrika Korps consisted of 15th and 21st Panzer Divisions and the recently arrived 'Special Service Afrika Division' (Div ZBV),[6] a small infantry division later known as 90th Light. Rommel's thoughts were concentrated on planning an attack on Tobruk, led by the Afrika Korps. It was to be delivered from the south-east, and the Korps, which had been engaged in intensive training, was in the area round Gambut. The Italian infantry divisions, other than Savona, manned positions surrounding Scobie's[7] 70th Division in Tobruk, and Gambara's 20th Mobile Corps had Ariete in the area of Bir Gubi, 25 miles south of El Adem, and the recently arrived Trieste Motorized Division at Bir Hacheim, 30 miles further west. Rommel had 174 tanks in his two panzer divisions (139 Mark III and 35 Mark IV), excluding light tanks. Gambara had 146 Italian M13s, the effectiveness of which was generally discounted. Rommel's strength lay, not in tanks only, but in his formidable anti-tank guns, the 50mm, effective against British tanks at a longer range than the guns of the same calibre in the Mark III tank, and the 88mm, which had caused such trouble in *Battleaxe*. Twenty-three of the latter were in the frontier defences to support Savona Division, and 12 were with the Afrika Korps, which also had ninety-six 50mms.

In Eighth Army, Godwin-Austen, in 13th Corps, had Messervy's 4th Indian Division in the positions round Halfaya, which it had occupied since *Battleaxe*, and Freyberg's[8] 2nd New Zealand Division, recovered from its unpleasant experience in Greece and Crete. They were not motorized and were dependent on the provision of 3-ton troop-carrying lorries for movement. To support them, he had Watkins's[9] 1st Army Tank Brigade. While Messervy faced Savona's defences and pinned them down, Freyberg was to move round their southern flank at Sidi Omar and envelop them from the rear. That done, both divisions would clear the area westward, including Bardia itself, to join up with Norrie who by this time, it was assumed, would have defeated the enemy armour and joined hands with Scobie to raise the siege of Tobruk.

Norrie's other worries were the training of 1st South African Division and the state of the armour. Brink's[10] division, which had not had any serious opposition to contend with in its march from Nairobi to Addis Abbaba, had been employed digging the defences of Mersa Matruh. This combined with delays in completing the issue of its transport (it was to be a wholly motorized division), left little time or opportunity in which to train in the novelties of desert warfare. As the proposed date of Operation *Crusader*, 18 November, drew near, Brink began to be alarmed and tried to get the date postponed. Auchinleck had had enough trouble with Churchill already over postponements and could certainly not afford more. Norrie threatened Brink that 4th Indian Division would change places with him, if he were not prepared to start in time. Brink gave way, which for all concerned was probably a great pity, as Messervy's was the only really experienced infantry division in the desert.

Although Norrie's total of tanks by mid-November was impressive, numbers alone did not tell the whole story. Seventh Armoured Brigade had experienced units (7th Hussars and 6th Royal Tanks), but their total of 168 tanks included 71 of the old A13 cruisers, the same number of the newer A15 Crusaders, and even 26 of the old A10s, so infirm that they had to be carried to battle on transporters. In support were 16 25-pounders of 4th RHA and a company of 2nd Rifle Brigade, with a troop each of anti-tank and light anti-aircraft guns. Twenty-second Armoured Brigade, advance guard of Norrie's 1st Armoured Division, consisted of three completely green yeomanry regiments, 3rd and 4th County of London Yeomanry and 2nd Royal Gloucestershire Hussars. They had 158 Crusaders, but, as they had all to be modified on arrival in the Middle East, little time had been left for training. Only eight 25-pounders of 4th RHA were available to support them with a company also of 1st KRRC (60th). Fourth Armoured Brigade, back to its old rôle as a cruiser brigade, also had experienced units in the 8th Hussars, 3rd and 5th Royal Tanks. Although its 165 new American Stuarts were highly thought of, they suffered a grave tactical disadvantage in their short range of only 40 miles. Their training had also been interrupted by a false alarm over the wear in their rubber-faced tracks. Norrie therefore had 491 tanks, and his were not the only British ones. Watkins's 1st Army Tank Brigade with 13 Corps had 132 infantry tanks, 8th Royal Tanks with Valentines, the 42nd and 44th with Matildas. Inside Tobruk itself 4th Royal Tanks had arrived to join the 32 old cruisers and 25 light tanks of 1st Royal Tanks and the Matilda squadron of the 7th, bringing the total of the last to 69. The total British tank strength (excluding light tanks) was therefore 724, of which 201 were the thickly armoured infantry tanks and 523 cruisers of various kinds, the gun of all of them being the 2-pounder (or the American 37mm, its equivalent), which was slightly superior in armour-piercing performance at this time to the guns carried in the principal German tanks, the Marks III and IV. As far as armour was concerned, the infantry tanks were better protected than any German tank. The cruisers also had an advantage, except where the Germans had bolted on additional plates; but at this time these did not prevent the 2-pounder from penetrating at ranges up to 500 yards, and probably up to 1000.[11]

Reference to Norrie's other worries brings us to his principal one, which centred on the restrictions imposed by Cunningham on how he should carry out his task. In the initial stages of planning, Cunningham had stressed that

Norrie's primary task was to destroy the enemy armour, which was to be 'hemmed in and not allowed to escape'. The relief of Tobruk was to be 'incidental to the plan'. Norrie wished to keep his three armoured brigades together and move them 'to a central position from which he could strike in any direction'. As planning proceeded, Norrie changed this idea to one in which he would move straight for Tobruk. Cunningham opposed this, largely because Freyberg had objected strongly to the possibility of his division being moved round the flank of the frontier defences before Rommel's armour had been decisively defeated and when all Norrie's tanks might be a long way away. The result was a compromise. Norrie's right-hand brigade, Gatehouse's 4th, would initially keep within supporting distance of Freyberg. Cunningham would move with Norrie on the approach march. From the enemy's reaction to it, he expected to be able to judge Rommel's intentions by the first evening, at which time 30th Corps would be 'in a central battle position round Gabr Saleh. The armoured cars would push forward from there to find the enemy, and 13th Corps, the left flank of which would be protected by 4th Armoured Brigade, would do the absolute minimum until the reaction of the enemy armour had been ascertained.'[12]

Operation *Crusader*, the biggest armoured operation the British army had hitherto been involved in, was launched during the night of 17/18 November and took Rommel completely by surprise. Cunningham travelled with Norrie as planned, but by the end of the day of the 18th, there did not appear to have been any reaction by Rommel, and it was not at all clear where his panzer divisions were or what they were doing. At about that time von Ravenstein, commander of 21st Panzer Division, had at last realized that British tanks were near Gabr Saleh – they were from Davy's[13] 7th Armoured Brigade – and proposed to order his tank regiment to oppose them. Crüwell agreed and ordered Neumann-Silkow's 15th Panzer Division, in a rest area north of Gambut, to move south above the escarpment. Rommel, still intent on his attack on Tobruk, disagreed, saying: 'We must not lose our nerve.' In a message to Gambara, he talked of 'intensive reconnaissance' next day.

Intensive reconnaissance was also the theme of Cunningham's orders for the 19th. Although as anxious as Norrie to get to Sidi Rezegh as soon as possible and launch the operation to link up with Scobie, he did not let him commit all his tanks in that direction until he had some idea where Rommel's were. He could not disregard Freyberg's fear that all Norrie's tanks would disappear into the desert and that Rommel's would then appear behind them and have Godwin-Austen's vulnerable infantry at their mercy. Norrie's orders for the 19th, based on Cunningham's directive, were for Gott to send

Scott-Cockburn's[14] 22nd Armoured Brigade to 'reconnoitre towards' Bir Gubi and 'be prepared to occupy it'. Brink was 'to be prepared to relieve' Scott-Cockburn there, so that the latter could move to join 7th Armoured Brigade, who had been told to 'reconnoitre towards Sidi Rezegh and be prepared to occupy it'. Gatehouse, to conform to the commitment to Godwin-Austen, was not to move 4th Armoured Brigade west of a line running north from just west of Gabr Saleh. This would result in Gott's three armoured brigades being separated, 22nd 20 miles from 7th, and the latter 35 from 4th, which would itself be 30 from 22nd. These tentative moves, dispersing the three armoured brigades before the enemy's main force had been detected, were to have a baleful effect on future events. It would have been better if Norrie, as he wished, had been allowed to press on with at least 7th and 22nd Brigades to Sidi Rezegh, even if 4th had to be held in reserve in case the Afrika Korps appeared on the right flank.

Rommel was not doing any better. He made no move until the afternoon of the 19th, when 5th Tank Regiment of 21st Panzer Division (85 Mark IIIs and IVs), commanded by Stephan, was sent south to Gabr Saleh to deal with the tanks reported by the reconnaisance unit there, after which it was to turn south-east to near Sidi Omar. Fifteenth Panzer was to move to the area south-west of Gambut. This would separate 21st Panzer's tank regiment from the rest of the division and take it 30 miles away from that of the 15th. In an attempt to find out where the German tanks were, Gatehouse detached one of his regiments, 3rd Royal Tanks, to support the armoured cars in driving away the German reconnaissance unit that was preventing them from penetrating further north. It was only too successful and one of its squadrons got as far north as the escarpment north-west of Sidi Azeiz. This meant that when, in the late afternoon, Stephan reached the area of Gabr Saleh, Gatehouse had not only not been warned by armoured cars of his approach, but he was without one of his own regiments. Observing the customary dispersion, the latter were ten miles apart and one of them, the 8th Hussars, had to bear the brunt of a two-hour engagement with Stephan which lasted until dark, losing 20 tanks. Fifth Royal Tanks, brought over to help them, lost three. Twelve of these 23 were fit again two days later. Unfortunately they exaggerated the damage they had done in return, claiming 19 certain and 26 possible enemy tanks knocked out, while in fact Stephan lost only 3 knocked out and 4 disabled. Thus began a cumulative process of over-estimating the losses inflicted, which was to have a serious effect later.

Meanwhile, on Norrie's left, 22nd Armoured Brigade had come up against Ariete at Bir Gubi and, although inflicting damage on the Italians, had suffered a bloody nose, reporting that they were down to half their strength as a result of a combination of losses (25 tanks) and breakdowns. New to the desert, their administration was far from efficient: they were in constant trouble with their fuel supplies and were somewhat disorganized. Ariete had not been dislodged. Davy's 7th Armoured Brigade had had a better day, having reached Sidi Rezegh almost unopposed. Norrie was all for exploiting this opportunity, but Cunningham hesitated. He could not make out what Rommel was up to, and decided to return to his own headquarters in the hope of receiving better information from sources not available to him while he was with Norrie.

Rommel's picture of the situation was no clearer. Third Royal Tank's adventure helped to mislead him and Crüwell. Gatehouse had in fact recalled them, but the events of the day led Crüwell to assume that Norrie's armour was in two groups, one near Sidi Azeiz and the other at Gabr Saleh. Rommel had given him only the vaguest of orders: to destroy the enemy in rear of the frontier defences, and then move on to deal with those in the area of the frontier itself. Navarini would look after Tobruk, while Gambara protected the flank from any wide outflanking movement, the threat of which had been raised by reports of a British force in the area of Giarabub, 130 miles south of Bir Gubi. Crüwell decided to use Sümmermann's Div ZBV to eject Davy from Sidi Rezegh airfield, and to concentrate his two panzer divisions to deal, first with the tank group at Gabr Saleh, and then with the one believed to be near Sidi Azeiz. That decision, which owed nothing to Rommel, seized the initiative from Cunningham, who had forfeited it by his hesitation, an advantage Crüwell was to hold for several days, only to be deprived of it by Rommel's rashness on 24 November.

Twentieth November was an important day. Gott moved Campbell's Support Group up to join Davy, and under the mistaken impression that there was little between them and Tobruk, pressed Norrie to urge Cunningham to order Scobie to launch his sortie towards them. Norrie passed this on, but Cunningham hesitated once more, this time with some justification. Air reconnaissance late on 19 November having detected westward movement of vehicles from the frontier towards Tobruk, the impression was formed at Headquarters Eighth Army that Rommel was trying to extricate his forces from east of Tobruk and move them further west, an impression which was to persist for some days and led to a serious misappreciation of Rommel's intentions. Whether as part of this plan or not, wireless intercept revealed that Crüwell was concentrating his two panzer divisions and intending to attack Gatehouse. Cunningham warned Norrie of this danger, as a result of which the latter ordered 22nd Armoured Brigade to move east to join the 4th, handing over the task of masking Ariete to Brink with Pienaar's 1st South African Brigade. Later in the day he gave Norrie the authority to pass the codeword to Scobie to start his sortie next day, 21 November.

For a number of reasons, including difficulties with the South Africans, Scott-Cockburn's move to join Gatehouse, a distance of 20 miles, took a long time. Fortunately Crüwell was having difficulties too, 21st Panzer Division's supply arrangements having become disorganized, partly due to the previous activities of 3rd Royal Tanks. In spite of the warning and Crüwell's slowness in moving, Gatehouse appears to have been taken by surprise when 15th Panzer Division's leading tanks appeared on his left flank at 1630 hrs and attacked 3rd Royal Tanks: 21st Panzer, still awaiting fuel, had been left behind. As usual his units were widely separated, and it was only by a tactical withdrawal, which brought 3rd and 5th Royal Tanks closer together, that he brought matters under control. A fierce battle continued until after dark, by which time Scott-Cockburn, with 100 Crusaders, had appeared on the left flank. Gatehouse's losses amounted to 26, reducing his tank strength to 97. He claimed to have knocked out 30 of the enemy, but the Afrika Korps reported no losses.

The situation at the end of the day did not look too unfavourable to Norrie. Gott, with Davy and Campbell, was concentrated at Sidi Rezegh, ready to launch an attack to join hands with Scobie, and Norrie ordered Brink to send his 5th Brigade to reinforce him. Gatehouse and Scott-Cockburn, with about 200 tanks, appeared not only to have held Crüwell's tanks, but to have inflicted significant casualties on them: 45–50 over two days out of their original 174. Norrie's orders to Gott were for 4th and 22nd Armoured Brigades to renew the battle with the Afrika Korps tanks in the morning, and pursue them relentlessly if they withdrew. Seventh Support Group, supported by Davy's tanks, was to attack the Sidi Rezegh ridge and thrust north to join Scobie's attack, directed towards Ed Duda. One of the problems of this was that Gott had two quite separate operations on his hands, each involving two brigades – the Sidi Rezegh one involved three, when 5th South African Brigade reached him. Rommel and Crüwell had meanwhile at last woken up to the threat posed by Davy and Campbell. They realized that the group thought to be near Sidi Azeiz did not exist, and assumed that Neumann-Silkow had trounced Gatehouse, eliminating him as a threat. Von Ravenstein's 21st was ordered to move south to join Neumann-Silkow during the night, and for both of them to move at dawn fast north-west to deal with the situation at Sidi Rezegh. Once that were accomplished, Crüwell would at last have his corps concentrated.

Unfortunately, on this crucial 21 November, things went Rommel's way and not Norrie's. Scobie's thrust at first went well, although his casualties, both in tanks and infantry, were heavy. Campbell found Div ZBV's position too hard a nut to crack, in spite of a gallant attack by his riflemen, supported by 42 guns and 6th Royal Tanks, who, having penetrated beyond the ridge, had almost all their tanks knocked out, probably by four 88mms brought up personally by Rommel. Gatehouse and Scott-Cockburn had failed either to engage 15th and 21st Panzer Divisions or to pursue them relentlessly, when Crüwell started his move towards Sidi Rezegh at 0720 hrs. Unfortunately this was interpreted as the flight of a beaten and battered foe, and the urgency of preventing them from joining the battle at Sidi Rezegh does not seem to have been appreciated, except by Davy, who, handing over command of 6th Royal Tanks to Campbell, faced about and by 0820 hrs clashed with 15th Panzer, just as the riflemen launched their attack on the Sidi Rezegh ridge.

For the rest of the day, Davy and Campbell, with no help from Gatehouse or Scott-Cockburn, fought a gallant battle round Sidi Rezegh, at the end of which Davy had only 15 tanks left and Campbell's infantry, particularly 1st KRRC, had suffered heavy casualties, as had some of his artillery. Gatehouse had been kept out of the fight by 21st Panzer and was stationary for most of the day in a position which was to become familiar to his brigade – Bir er Reghem, ten miles south-east of Sidi Rezegh; while Scott-Cockburn had wandered about the desert, at least trying, although unsuccessfully, to come to Davy's aid. Fifth South African Brigade had been stopped by Gott at 1000 hrs, when 12 miles south of the airfield, as he saw no point in this inexperienced and vulnerable formation getting involved in the battle, dominated by tanks, at that stage. Scobie's thrust was stalled in the salient he had created, three miles deep and wide, with its apex six miles north of Sidi Rezegh.

It was very late in the day of 21 November before the realities of this situation became clear to Norrie, and then to Cunningham. Having been persuaded by Norrie to order Scobie to start his sortie, and having been given a rosy picture of the situation that morning, Cunningham became increasingly anxious at the slowness of Norrie's attempts to link up with Tobruk. He pressed him to use the whole of 1st South African Division, and even offered also 6th New Zealand Brigade, which at that time was on its way north to the Trigh Capuzzo, west of Sidi Azeiz. He assumed that it could turn west along the Trigh to join Norrie. The latter, not knowing where it was and feeling that he had enough infantry for the moment, declined the offer. The picture painted to Cunningham by his staff that evening was that some 60 German tanks were surrounded by Gott's three armoured brigades and Armstrong's[15] 5th South African infantry south-east of Sidi Rezegh, which was held by Campbell. Meanwhile Ariete had not stirred from Bir Gubi, and Freyberg had started to move round behind Savona's frontier defences, which Messervy was attacking from the south. To Cunningham the situation looked promising. His concern was that Norrie should redouble his efforts to join Scobie. The key to this was to establish both 1st South African Division and all Gott's brigades in the vital area of the escarpments north and south of Sidi Rezegh airfield.

This false picture of the situation was shared by Rommel and Crüwell. The former believed that it was only through his personal intervention on the battlefield that a junction between Cunningham's forces and Tobruk had been prevented. Crüwell thought that he was surrounded on all sides and wished to escape from the trap by moving east to the area south of Gambut, where he could join his supply echelons. Rommel however ordered him to hold a defensive line along the escarpment running east from El Adem. Crüwell, without informing his superior, compromised by sending 21st Panzer westward towards Belhamed and 15th eastward to the Trigh Capuzzo south of Gambut. By dawn on 22 November these moves had not been completed, and Gott's men were glad to see the tail of both divisions disappear over the escarpment in the early morning, a move once more interpreted as the retreat of a defeated enemy. In spite of the weakness of 7th Armoured Brigade and the casualties Campbell had suffered, the prospect looked favourable when Cunningham visited Norrie and urged him to concentrate Brink's brigades at Sidi Rezegh, while the Guards Brigade[16] relieved Pienaar[17] of the task of masking Ariete at Bir Gubi.

Both Rommel and Crüwell, separately, became concerned at the concentration of Gott's forces which they saw to the south. Without reference to Crüwell, Rommel at about midday personally ordered von Ravenstein, who had expected a defensive rôle at Belhamed, to attack and throw Campbell's men off the northern Sidi Rezegh escarpment, his tanks to come in from the western flank. Independently, an hour later, Crüwell ordered Neumann-Silkow to return to where he had come from and attack the concentration from the eastern flank.

By chance and unknown to each other, Rommel and Crüwell had thus devised a pincer movement extremely dangerous to Campbell and Davy's tiny remnant, reinforced at two o'clock by Scott-Cockburn. Had it been co-ordinated in timing, it would probably have proved disastrous to 7th Armoured Division. If, on the other hand, Scobie had continued his thrust from Tobruk that day, it would seriously have interfered with von Ravenstein; but he had been told to take no action until the afternoon, by which time it was hoped that 30 Corps might be at Ed Duda, an eventuality which Gott realized early in the day he could not achieve.[18]

Twenty-first Panzer was quick off the mark and delivered a vigorous attack soon after Scott-Cockburn had moved into the arena. Gott ordered Gatehouse to move to their aid, but by 1545 hrs, before he had got far, Campbell's infantry were forced off the ridge and von Ravenstein's tanks were on the airfield. Gatehouse was uncertain of the situation and reluctant to allow his leading regiments, 3rd and 5th Royal Tanks, to get involved in the mêlée, to the fury of Campbell who led some of them off personally to fight the enemy tanks. Gatehouse accepted the recommendation of his two commanding officers that the only way to sort out the confusion was to withdraw to the south-east out of the dust and smoke. By this time, when it was nearly dark, 15th Panzer, which had not started to move until 1530 hrs, appeared from that direction, and soon became embroiled with 8th Hussars and Gatehouse's headquarters.

While this battle had been raging, Norrie had been urging Brink to move his brigades up to the escarpment south of the airfield. Pienaar refused to budge from Bir Gubi until the Guards had completed a take-over of his positions, and Armstrong had advanced cautiously until he met opposition three miles south of his objective, point 178. Meanwhile Barrowclough's[19] 6th New Zealand Brigade was making good progress westward along the Trigh Capuzzo towards the area in which 15th Panzer Division had spent most of the day. The situation at the end of this day, 22 November, looked much less promising than it had at the beginning. It was made worse by the confusion and loss of control caused by 15th Panzer Division's brush with Headquarters 4th Armoured Brigade. Although Gatehouse himself was not present at the time, the result was that neither Gott nor Norrie knew what had happened to his brigade, which, owing to the breakdown of control, remained, with its 100 tanks, completely ineffective for 24 hours. Davy's brigade had already been reduced to ineffectiveness by casualties and Scott-Cockburn's 22nd had only 30 tanks fit for action.

Reduced as Norrie's effective tank strength was, it was not as weak as Rommel now believed. Under the impression that one more blow would remove the threat of Norrie's forces altogether, he planned a pincer movement for 23 November, the German *Totensonntag*. At 0700 hrs Crüwell, with both panzer divisions, was to move south-west, with the main effort on his left, around the rear of Norrie's forces south of Sidi Rezegh. An hour later, Ariete, still not under his command, was to move north-east from Bir Gubi to form the other arm of the pincer. These orders did not reach Crüwell until 0430 hrs on the 23 November, more than 12 hours since he had last seen

Rommel. He had already issued somewhat similar orders of his own. Von Ravenstein, with Sümmermann's infantry as well as his own, was to hold Sidi Rezegh, sending his tanks to join 15th Panzer Division, which would then move round Gott's rear to join Ariete, after which both would drive the remnants of Norrie's forces north into the jaws of von Ravenstein. He left his headquarters just before first light to join Neumann-Silkow, shortly before Barrowclough appeared from the east and bumped into it. By 0730 hrs 21st Panzer's tank regiment had not arrived, and Crüwell and Neumann-Silkow set off without them. Their move took them through an area littered with vehicles, some of them Campbell's and Davy's units, others their supply echelons and those of Armstrong's brigade. Brushing aside the attempts of the former to engage them, and not bothering to stop and inflict damage on the latter, they continued on and disappeared into the desert to the south-west. Uncertain what this might portend, Gott concentrated on trying to get 4th Armoured Brigade into action again, while Norrie urged Pienaar on and tried to get in touch with Barrowclough. Armstrong had not reached the escarpment, but had dug himself in where he was, three miles short of it, reinforced by some of Campbell's guns and Gatehouse's motor infantry battalion, 2nd Scots Guards. German infantry from Div ZBV were on the escarpment north of them, and they were under fire from Böttcher's heavy artillery.

By this time everybody was tired and welcomed the lull in activity after the early morning excitement. It was the lull before the storm. Having had some difficulty in forming up his force, at 1500 hrs Crüwell drove north with Ariete on his left, and within a quarter of an hour was attacking Armstrong's position. Although Gott tried to help him, the activities of the much reduced 22nd Armoured Brigade from the west and of the combined efforts of Davy, Campbell and two of Gatehouse's regiments from the east made little impact. By 1600 hrs all was over and most of the brigade, including Armstrong himself, taken prisoner. Neither side realized for some time what losses they had inflicted on the Afrika Korps: 72 out of their remaining 162 tanks, so that Crüwell had only 90 left of the 249 (both figures including light tanks) with which he had started five days before. He also suffered heavy human casualties, particularly among company and battalion commanders.

Crüwell, who had himself narrowly escaped capture, assumed that he had now accounted for all the major elements of Norrie's forces. His own were disorganized and he was out of touch both with his divisional commanders and with Rommel. His plan for 24 November was to get his Korps together again, recover and repair as many of his tanks as he could, and mop up the remnants of Norrie's formations between the Trigh Capuzzo and the Trigh el Abd. Rommel's plan was more ambitious: a thrust south from Sidi Rezegh which would then turn east to Sidi Omar, encircling all the forces north of that thrust. Apparently not realizing that Freyberg's troops were west of the frontier defences, he planned to continue east from Sidi Omar and encircle 13th Corps, which he assumed would then be between the Afrika Korps and Savona. It was an astonishingly bold, indeed a reckless, plan, which was to prove his undoing. He told his chief of staff, Colonel Westphal, who was to remain at El Adem, that he expected to be back from this jaunt by the end of the day, or, if not, early in the morning of 25 November. The first that Crüwell heard of this plan was when he met Von Ravenstein somewhere near Belhamed at o6oo hrs, two hours after Rommel had personally given these orders to his divisional commanders. The job of commander of the Afrika Korps under Rommel was not an easy one. He did not just breathe down his subordinate's neck: he blew right past him.

By 22 November Cunningham had become seriously concerned, as he saw the initiative slipping away from him. However, while things had been going badly for Norrie, Godwin-Austen was doing well. Messervy was steadily mopping up Savona and Freyberg was progressing westward without meeting serious opposition, although Barrowclough was held up east of Sidi Rezegh. He therefore decided to transfer to Godwin-Austen the task of joining up with Scobie, while Norrie, handing 1st South African Division over to 13th Corps, would protect Godwin-Austen's southern flank and 'continue the destruction of the enemy armour'. The events of the 23rd prevented that tidy concept from being implemented. It came as a shock to Godwin-Austen to discover that the enemy armour had not, as he had been led to believe, already been destroyed before he sent Freyberg off into the blue. However he took a more robust view of the situation than did Cunningham. When the latter heard on 23 November that 7th Armoured Brigade had virtually ceased to exist, that 22nd was reduced to 30 tanks, and that nobody knew what had happened to the 4th, he proposed that 13th Corps should halt any further westward movement, until 30th had been reorganized and its tank strength been improved. Godwin-Austen felt that his corps was in a good state, and was all for pushing on. He was reinforced in this view by a radio conversation with Norrie, who, in the midday lull of *Totensonntag*, had said he was 'perfectly able to deal with the situation for the rest of the day in the event of an enemy counterattack'. Cunningham let him have his way, but remained much concerned and asked Auchinleck to come up and discuss it. His chief of staff, Galloway,[20] equally concerned at both the physical and the mental state of his commander, also rang GHQ to make sure that the Commander-in-Chief came. He arrived at Headquarters Eighth Army with Tedder that evening.

By that time the fate of 5th South African Brigade was known, but Auchinleck had no doubt that the robust (if, in the case of Norrie, over-optimistic) attitude of Cunningham's commanders should be supported. He was convinced that Rommel must have difficulties of his own (Crüwell would have agreed with him), and he told Cunningham to 'continue his offensive with the object of recapturing Sidi Rezegh and joining hands with Tobruk garrison'. Cunningham stuck to his decision that this should be primarily the task of Godwin-Austen, who would also take Scobie under command. Norrie was to reorganize his corps immediately, 'provide all possible protection' to 1st South African Division (now 1st South African and 22nd Guards Brigades) and 'be prepared to go to the help of the New Zealand Division in the event of a concentrated enemy tank attack' and 'not to neglect his rear'. The surprising comment was added that the tank strengths reported by 30th Corps at the end of 22 November (i.e. the ones that had caused Cunningham such concern) made 'comfortable allowance for this without prejudice to the main rôle of armoured forces which is to destroy tanks'. To implement these orders, it seemed to Norrie that his plan for the 24th should be to concentrate Gott's 7th Armoured Division in the area south-east of Sidi Rezegh, while Brink used Pienaar's brigade, which had not moved far from its original position east of Bir Gubi, to keep an eye on Ariete. The general impression in 30th Corps was that it was going to have a short rest in which to pull itself together, while the burden of the fighting was transferred to the 13th.

Rommel dealt a sharp blow to that illusion in mid-morning. Increasingly frustrated at the delay in getting things going, he issued a direct order to the tank regiment of 21 Panzer to start moving at 1040 hrs. This set off a train of extraordinary events. His route took him between Norrie's combat forma-tions, but, following the Trigh el Abd, the long strung-out column of the Afrika Korps, followed by Ariete, dispersed in near-panic most of Norrie's supply echelons and his own main headquarters, which eventually finished up near Sidi Azeiz. By the greatest stroke of good fortune, they swept past his principal supply dumps and logistic units. Norrie himself (with the author) was at Gott's headquarters, and he had been joined by Cunningham, who had flown up to discuss the situation. He managed to get back to his aircraft just in time, reaching his headquarters at midday to find that Auchinleck had spent the morning turning the previous night's order into a formal instruction. It was full of stirring phrases such as 'relentlessly using all resources down to the last tank' and 'to the limit of endurance', 'determined effort', 'utmost boldness', 'worth immense risks, which will be taken', but contained no more of practical value than the simple directives of the previous evening.[21] Cunningham got back into his aircraft to fly to Godwin-Austen, who was as pugnacious as ever. On the return flight, he saw below him the eastward flow of vehicles, some those of the Afrika Korps, but most his own.

It is not surprising that he was depressed. Air reconnaisance at dawn revealed that most of the Afrika Korps was near Sheferzen on the frontier wire, 30 miles north of his own headquarters and 25 from the only remaining forward airfield. There were practically no combat units between it and the supply depôts and railhead on which the logistic support of his whole army depended. At about midday Auchinleck and Tedder took off for Cairo, the former leaving behind a personal message to all ranks of Eighth Army, full of stirring phrases, which if it ever reached the front line troops (which it probably did not), would have been received with the customary cynicism with which the British soldier down the ages has treated such communications. Whatever effect Auchinleck may have expected his message to produce on the troops of Eighth Army, he had no faith that its commander could produce the results he wanted. His lack of confidence in Cunningham was supported by Tedder, Coningham,[22] the Desert Air Force commander and Galloway, It was clear that he must go, and go quickly. The problem was to find a successor. Auchinleck had already turned down 'Jumbo' Wilson, when Churchill had suggested him as Eighth Army's first commander, and felt no more inclined to appoint that ponderous figure to the post than he had before. If he were to promote Godwin-Austen or Norrie, there would be the problem of which, and of finding a successor to whomever he chose. Both were involved in the battle: Godwin-Austen had no previous experience of handling armoured formations and Norrie's performance hitherto had not been particularly impressive. He did not feel he could wait until a new commander arrived from England, who, in any case, would be completely new to the situation and its problems. His choice fell on his Deputy Chief of the General Staff, Major-General Neil Ritchie. He had come from England to join Wavell's staff shortly before the latter was dismissed, having been well-known to him as a brother officer in The Black Watch. There was no doubt that he would adopt a robust, optimistic attitude: he was immediately available and fully aware of Auchinleck's views. Ritchie was reluctant to accept. His only personal experience of desert warfare dated from the First World War campaign in Mesopotamia, and he had no experience of command in action. He thought that Auchinleck should himself assume direct command, until a successor could arrive from England, as Churchill himself suggested.[23]

Ritchie arrived at Headquarters Eighth Army in the late afternoon of 26 November, a few hours after Auchinleck's chief of staff, Arthur Smith,[24] had delivered to Cunningham his letter of dismissal. He found that the situation had been largely restored, not by any direct contribution of Auchinleck's, but by the toughness of the New Zealanders and the determination of Freyberg, egged on by Godwin-Austen, to push westward towards Tobruk – this in spite of the antics of the Afrika Korps in the area of the frontier of which in fact they appeared to be almost entirely ignorant. With Rommel and Crüwell constantly at cross purposes, often out of touch with each other and their subordinates, and cut off from their principal logistic area by the presence of the New Zealanders round Gambut (who had failed to locate it), the Afrika Korps spent two fruitless days manoeuvring on both sides of the frontier defences, now partially occupied, not by Savona, but by 4th Indian Division. As they pulled back into the area west of the defences, partly in order to obtain supplies from Bardia, the position of Freyberg and of Godwin-Austen's headquarters (to which Norrie's had become attached, although he was not with it) became increasingly precarious. Freyberg himself, with his 4th and 6th Brigades, strongly supported by Watkins's Matildas, was forward, battling his way at increasing cost against Sümmer-mann and Böttcher towards Scobie, who renewed attempts to break out towards him. The closer Freyberg got, the greater was the danger to his rear, and, on 27 November, his 5th Brigade, round Sidi Azeiz, was attacked, the headquarters and one battalion being overrun by 15th Panzer Division, not many hours after his 4th Brigade had at last made contact with Scobie's men.

Westphal had become increasingly concerned at the threat posed by Freyberg and sent a series of appeals to Rommel to bring the Afrika Korps back to deal with it, appeals backed by Crüwell and Neumann-Silkow. Rommel was reluctant to abandon his adventure, but was finally convinced, and by the late morning of 27 November it was clear to Ritchie and Norrie that a major movement westward was taking place. This was misinterpreted at Headquarters Eighth Army as an attempt by Rommel to 'escape westward' and Ritchie urged Norrie to stop him. The latter, although his mind had turned towards a thrust to El Adem, which would loosen up the situation to help Freyberg and Scobie, was in a good position to do so. With his small tactical headquarters attached to Gott's, both having evaded Rommel's onrush, he had spent the two previous days reorganizing 7th Armoured Division. Davy's brigade was removed, the remaining cruiser tanks, 45 in number, being concentrated under Scott-Cockburn, while Gatehouse had 77 Stuarts. The former was protecting Freyberg's rear and was moved east to face the returning Afrika Korps, while Gatehouse was moved from north of Gabr Saleh to join him. Scott-Cockburn held Neumann-Silkow, who had 13 light and 37 medium (later reinforced by 9) tanks, for several hours, while Gatehouse attacked the flank; the two of them lost 19 tanks before darkness fell, when they drew off, Gatehouse five miles to the south and Scott-Cockburn rather further to the south-west.

For the sake of performing a nightly ritual, therefore, the fruits of the first occasion on which the British armour had been able to forestall the German, and concentrate against a portion of it, were thrown away. The important and favourable situation which it had gained, protecting the rear of 13 Corps and barring Rommel's return to intervene, was abandoned without a struggle. Neumann-Silkow was understandably surprised and relieved when he found it possible to move a further six miles west, south of the Sidi Rezegh escarpment, to Bir Sciafsciuf after dark. Here he was only a few miles south-west of the headquarters of 13 Corps and New Zealand Division, which had both moved westwards while the afternoon battle was in progress.[25]

The threat that this posed to Freyberg was not immediately appreciated. Ritchie was thinking in terms of preventing an escape: Godwin-Austen, Freyberg and Scobie were concentrating on opening up the corridor to Tobruk and sorting out logistics. Norrie was concerned to move Pienaar up to join Freyberg while Gott undid the damage caused by his armoured brigades letting the Afrika Korps move west during the night. But attempts by the latter to do so were repulsed by Ariete and the infantry of 15th Panzer Division, neither the tanks of the division nor those of 21st Panzer being engaged, the latter being out of fuel as usual. The threat was realized late in the day when Neumann-Silkow's troops overran a New Zealand field hospital not far from Freyberg's headquarters. As a result, Godwin-Austen moved his headquarters and most of Freyberg's transport and supply into Tobruk.

As usual, Rommel and Crüwell had differing plans as to how to attack Freyberg, and in the event neither 15th nor 21st Panzer Division did what either of their superiors wished on 29 November. Von Ravenstein was captured, reconnoitring for an attack on Freyberg's rear from the east, and his division made no progress against the determined resistance of 4th New Zealand and 1st Army Tank Brigades. Neumann-Silkow went further west than he was meant to, and found himself engaged in a fight with two of Scobie's battalions, supported by all 24 of his remaining Matildas. Receiving a bloody nose and misunderstanding his orders, he withdrew to El Adem after dark. Rommel's two panzer divisions were now widely separated, with only Ariete between them. Norrie had been doing all he could to prod

Pienaar to get moving to join Freyberg from the south, but his intention was frustrated by a combination of Pienaar's reluctance to enter into an arena in which enemy tanks might be active and misunderstandings in messages passed between the two. Norrie's orders for 30 November to Gott and the latter's to Gatehouse, under whose command all 7th Armoured Division's 120 tanks were now concentrated, were not conducive to decisive action by the latter to improve Freyberg's situation. Norrie told Gott to 'harass and destroy the enemy as opportunity offered and to protect 1st South African Brigade which was under orders to advance and regain Point 175 from the enemy'. This was passed on to Gatehouse as 'to maintain the corridor to NZ Div near Point 175 and protect 1st SA Brigade'. Gatehouse was not the one to give his orders a more offensive flavour.

Thus the powerful 4th Armoured Brigade spent all day bickering with Ariete, of whose inferiority in both quality and quantity of tanks there can be no doubt at all, and did not even move it away from the south of Sidi Rezegh, let alone inflict any serious casualties, although Captain Doyle of 5th Royal Tanks claimed to have destroyed sixteen M13s. As this tank battle, which lasted all day, blocked the route to Point 175, Pienaar's interpretation of his orders was to send one battalion up to Armstrong's old battlefield; but when it was shelled there, it was told to return and no further move was made.[26]

Over-riding objections from Crüwell, who was concerned at the weak state of his divisions, Rommel renewed the attack on Freyberg, to be delivered by the 14 medium and 6 light tanks of 21st Panzer Division, now commanded by Böttcher, on 6th New Zealand Brigade at Sidi Rezegh from the southeast, while 15th Panzer, with 28 medium and 11 light, attacked from the west and Ariete completed the clearance of the escarpment west of Point 175. The attack was not launched until nearly 1600 hrs, after 6th Brigade had been subjected to heavy shelling almost all day. Barrowclough and Freyberg had been hoping for relief from Gatehouse and Pienaar, but none came, and when darkness fell soon after 1730 hrs, there was little left of the brigade, the survivors joining the 4th New Zealand Brigade at Belhamed. Crüwell renewed the attack with 15th Panzer Division soon after first light on 1 December. Acting on Norrie's orders, Gott, at 0400 hrs, had ordered Gatehouse to move at first light to 'reconnoitre the Sidi Rezegh area and counterattack enemy tanks at all costs'.[27] Gatehouse sent 5th Royal Tanks ahead to contact 6th Brigade, discover what the situation was and make a plan to deal with it.

The brigade was fired at from left and right as it drove down, feeling very much as if it were repeating the charge of the light brigade at Balaclava.

Their arrival raised great hopes, but its effect quickly evaporated in a cloud of misunderstanding. They saw their task as one of rescuing the New Zealanders and bringing them back the way they had come. Barrowclough's men hoped that Gatehouse would drive the enemy away; but, if withdrawal was to be the order of the day, they would join Freyberg and Inglis. The tanks knew that Point 175 was held by the enemy, and would not go that way. So the two parted, the dispirited and weary New Zealanders trudging off eastwards to join their comrades at Zaafran. Gatehouse's tanks stayed to see them away, and then returned themselves to their permanent station south-east of Sidi Rezegh, while 15th Panzer completed its capture of Belhamed, and 21st Panzer did nothing at all.[28]

Freyberg now decided to withdraw his division out of the battlefield area altogether without consulting Godwin-Austen, under whose command he was, although he may not have been in radio contact with him. He did consult Norrie, who agreed, but did not consult Ritchie, perhaps for the same reason. The latter had no alternative but to agree, when he was told.

Although Freyberg's withdrawal and the consequent closure of the corridor to Tobruk was a setback to Ritchie, it was in fact Rommel, and not he, who now faced defeat although Rommel refused to recognize the fact. The Afrika Korps had less than half of the tanks and two-thirds of the guns with which it had started the battle. Thanks to the action of the Royal Navy and the RAF, operating from Malta, his logistic situation was critical, and he had been warned by Bastico that there was no hope of any Italian reinforcement. To Crüwell's dismay he planned another return to the frontier, this time by the direct route. Crüwell thought that first priority should be given to eliminating the salient which Scobie's troops had established at Ed Duda. The result was a compromise, which split the Afrika Korps, 15th Panzer and Ariete setting off towards Bardia and Capuzzo, while 21st and Div ZBV attacked the salient.

Ritchie meanwhile had been planning a thrust towards El Adem, relieving 4th Indian Division on the frontier by 2nd South African, which had been concentrating at Mersa Matruh, and intending to use it, with all Norrie's tanks, to entice Rommel out into the open desert, where, it was erroneously assumed, he would be without the support of the anti-tank guns which 7th Armoured Division had found so troublesome, tucked into the crests of escarpments. Nevertheless it was a sound idea to thrust in that direction in order to regain the initiative, and it might force Rommel to leave the area east of Tobruk and open up access to Scobie. Prodded by Churchill, Auchinleck was scraping other areas of his command for reinforcements and, in order to satisfy himself that they would be properly used, he flew up to

Ritchie's headquarters on 1 December and stayed there for ten days, starting the practice of breathing down his subordinate's neck which was to affect Ritchie throughout his time in command. If Auchinleck was able to do this then, he should have been able to assume command himself, until a new commander came from England.

Norrie's attention was concentrated on the thrust towards El Adem, intending to clear up an Italian post at Bir Gubi as a preliminary operation. The attack on the post by 11th Indian Brigade in the early morning of 4 December was a failure, Gatehouse's 98 tanks a few miles away to the north-east not being engaged. One isolated Italian battalion, with a handful of tanks and one section of anti-tank guns, held up a whole corps and inflicted severe casualties on a complete infantry brigade, supported by a squadron of Valentine tanks. The brigade was an experienced one, and much of its failure can be attributed to attacking without previous reconnaisance after a long and complicated night march and to a lack of close co-operation with its supporting tanks and artillery. While this action was in train, Ritchie became concerned about 15th Panzer Division's threat to the frontier area, and, after flying into Tobruk to plan with Godwin-Austen a breakout by the garrison, he signalled Norrie, asking what he was doing about it and reminding him that it was his task to destroy enemy armour 'regardless of boundaries'. Norrie rightly protested that it was more important to stick to Ritchie's plan of keeping up pressure towards El Adem; but, having been ordered to 'move the centre of gravity back to where it was', he reluctantly ordered Gatehouse to move east for 20 miles. The anxieties of the staff at Ritchie's headquarters resulted in the despatch of an order in the early hours of the morning of the 5th, saying: 'Owing to enemy movements towards Bardia, it is considered essential to reduce frontier area prior to tackling Tobruk, thus reducing possibility of enemy refuelling from Bardia and operating in our rear. You will therefore be prepared to discuss plan for the operation with staff officer arriving today.' By the time it had been deciphered, it had become clear that Rommel had abandoned his eastward thrust. He was reacting to the presence of Norrie's forces near Bir Gubi, which he saw as a serious threat, although a renewed attempt by 11th Indian Brigade, supported by even fewer of Norrie's resources than before (although Gatehouse now had 136 tanks) was even less successful than the previous one. Rommel intended that, having dealt with Norrie, he would repeat his original jaunt down the Trigh el Abd to Sidi Omar. The next two days saw ineffective manoeuvring by both sides round Bir Gubi, each exaggerating the strength of the other and claiming to have engaged in fierce actions, when in fact little but skirmishes had taken place. Rommel's military fantasies were finally overcome by logistic realities, and on 7 December he gave orders for withdrawal, his Italian superiors at first refusing to accept its necessity. The argument continued for the next week, Bastico agreeing to hand over command of forces in Cyrenaica to Rommel, providing that he defended it as far east as Gazala. Rommel felt no confidence that he could hold Ritchie there, particularly as the air situation had changed markedly in Ritchie's favour. In the end Comando Supremo, having pointed out all the logistic factors which should limit Ritchie's ability to maintain any great strength far west of Tobruk, left the decision '*Al commandante in cito*' – to the commander on the spot – without specifying whom they meant.

Ritchie had decided that only one corps should be involved in following up the enemy's withdrawal, and that it should be Godwin-Austen's. Norrie protested that as his corps was designed for and experienced in mobile operations, he should have been preferred; but Ritchie pleaded logistic reasons. Auchinleck appears to have had some influence on the decision, as the progress of the Germans in Russia – they had reached Rostov – and the Japanese attacks in the Far East had already made him concerned about the rest of his command, and he wished to have a corps in reserve. Personal considerations no doubt played a part, Godwin-Austen, perhaps, having appeared to be more vigorous and aggressive than Norrie, the performance of whose corps had not been particularly impressive. Handing 4th Indian and 7th Armoured Divisions over to Godwin-Austen, Norrie, taking the South Africans with him, went back to mop up the frontier garrisons of Bardia and Sollum, whom Rommel had abandoned.

Whether Ritchie's choice was good or bad, the result was to impose the inevitable delay as command, and especially logistic, arrangements were reorganized. No effective attempt was made to interfere with Rommel's initial withdrawal to the Gazala-Alam Hamza position, and it was not until 13 December that a major operation was launched against it. Messervy's 4th Indian Division, without its 11th Brigade, which had not recovered from its experience at Bir Gubi, was to move round the southern flank, directed on Tmimi, while Gott, whose 90 tanks were all under Gatehouse, was to protect Messervy's open flank and raid Rommel's supply lines. It was an ambitious plan which failed as one of Messervy's brigades ran head-on into the remnants of Gambara's 20th Corps and the other into the Afrika Korps, while Gott's tanks were not within supporting distance of them. Godwin-Austen then tried to get Gott to outflank the enemy holding up Messervy, but supply problems and breakdowns prevented this from being implemented until 15 December, when Gatehouse was to carry out a wide turning movement, which would bring his tanks round to the rear of the force facing

Messervy. It would involve a trek of 70 miles, during which they would have to refuel twice. Admirable in concept, it failed to work out in practice. The desert 'going' was worse than expected, so that progress was slower and fuel consumption higher than planned. Gatehouse's tanks therefore had no influence on the battle that day. All the frontal attacks, made by Polish and New Zealand brigades, as well as by Messervy's two Indian ones, were repelled by the Italians, and 15th Panzer Division, with 23 out of Crüwell's total of 40 tanks, inflicted severe losses on 5th Indian Brigade. Godwin-Austen's hopes now rested on Gott, whom he ordered to attack from the rear the enemy facing Messervy next day. Petrol supply problems frustrated this, and, when, refuelled, Gatehouse's tanks came into contact with the Afrika Korps on Rommel's right flank, they made little progress. Nevertheless their fruitless manoeuvring had its impact on Rommel's mind. He told Cavallero, the Italian Chief of the General Staff, who had come to see him, that he had no alternative but to withdraw to Mechili and Tmimi as 'the enemy had enveloped the whole of his front'.

Cavallero did not object, and Rommel began to thin out, observed by Gott's forward troops as well as by air reconnaisance. He took a different tune when he saw Rommel again at 2300 hrs accompanied by Kesselring,[29] Bastico and Gambara. Rommel now demanded a complete withdrawal from Cyrenaica, and, after heated argument, a compromise was agreed, Cavallero insisting that no part of Cyrenaica should be given up unnecessarily. Rommel pretended to accept this, but, as soon as he detected that Gott's forces were advancing towards Mechili on 17 December, he ordered Crüwell all the way back to Agedabia, while the Italians withdrew to Benghazi. A few days later, he told the Italians not to stop at Benghazi, but continue on to the border of Tripolitania. He moved so quickly that Ritchie's attempts to bring about another Beda Fomm were frustrated, and all Rommel's forces got away, reinforced by 22 tanks which had been unloaded at Benghazi on 19 December from a convoy which unloaded another 23 at Tripoli on the same day. Two ships, containing another 45 between them, had been sunk *en route*. Gott's armoured cars entered Benghazi on 24 December, and on Christmas Day they made contact with Crüwell's outposts at Agedabia.

*   *   *

Operation *Crusader* thus came to an end in almost exactly the same place as had O'Connor's campaign against the Italians a year before. But, although it was undoubtedly a victory, and a notable one, it did not have the flavour of one, certainly not the aura of overwhelming success which had crowned the previous operation. The enemy's forces, although severely reduced in strength, had escaped the net; and the long-drawn-out, confused series of battles that had been fought, since Eighth Army had crossed the Libyan frontier-wire in such an exhilarated mood on 18 November, had left a taste of muddle and failure. Nevertheless Churchill's remark, 'Before Alamein we never had a victory. After Alamein we never had a defeat',[30] was as unfair to those who fought in *Crusader* as it was to those who defeated the Italians both in Libya and in East Africa. The two sides had started almost equal in numbers: Eighth Army with 118,000, their opponents with 119,000 – 65,000 German, 54,000 Italian. The British suffered rather more casualties: 2900 to 2300 killed, and 7300 to 6100 wounded; but a high proportion of Rommel's forces were captured. Their total of missing was 29,000 to the British 7500, 13,800 of their men having surrendered at Bardia and Halfaya. Tobruk had been relieved and the German and Italian forces flung out of Cyrenaica, the airfields of which were now available to give air cover to ships sailing to and from Malta. Auchinleck would have preferred to have destroyed Rommel's forces totally, and Ritchie might have done this if Rommel had given way to his superiors and attempted to hold or at least to impose delay on, Eighth Army in the Bulge of Cyrenaica. He might well then have suffered the same fate as the Italians the year before.

Why, in spite of this victory, was there a feeling of failure? It was that, with few exceptions, the enemy had consistently appeared to have had the better of the tactical battle. At the time, this was attributed to the superiority of his equipment, particularly of the German tanks over the British. 'Tank experts', like Hobart, particularly those who were not in the Middle East, blamed failure on the fact that senior commands were held by officers who did not understand tanks and how to 'handle' armour. Those who had taken part tended to blame it on the inability of infantry to defend themselves against tanks, with the result that tanks, instead of concentrating on their 'true' rôle, were dispersed or kept moving hither and thither to protect the infantry. Later post-war criticism has centred on faults of organization, of co-operation of all arms, and of both concept and method of command. In particular, failure to concentrate the armour has been highlighted as the principal error.

There is some truth in all these allegations, but not always in the way or to the degree that those who supported them maintained. The opposing tanks were not so very different in technical quality. The Matildas and Valentines, apart from their slow speed, were at a distinct advantage, with their thick armour, which was immune to all the enemy's tank guns at all but very short ranges. All British tanks were equipped with the 2-pounder gun, and the American Stuarts, with which 4th Armoured Brigade was initially equipped, carried the 37mm with an equivalent performance. Both were slightly superior in penetrative performance to the 50mm gun in the German Mark III, as well as to the low velocity 75mm in the Mark IV and the 47mm in the Italian tanks. At a range of 1000 yards, the 2-pounder could penetrate all parts of all the enemy tanks, except the turret front and one nine-inch-high vertical front plate of those German Mark IIIs – onto which additional plates had been bolted. The Official History [31] states: 'It is not possible to tell what proportion of up-armoured tanks fought during *Crusader*, but subsequent examination of the battlefield suggested that there had been a considerable number.' At that range, the 50mm in the Mark III could not penetrate the turret of the Crusader, but might just penetrate the front of its hull, as it might also the front of the Stuart, the side plates of which were thinner than those of the Crusader. It is clear, therefore, that the German tanks had no significant technical advantage over the British at that time.[32]

The Germans did, however, have a definite advantage in equipment in three fields: anti-tank guns, artillery and armoured personnel carriers. In their 88mms, of which however there were only 23 at the beginning of the operation, and in their 50mm Pak38 anti-tank guns, which had a significantly greater penetrative power than the 50mm gun in the Mark III tank, they had a real advantage, and the proportion of anti-tank guns to infantry was considerably higher than in the Eighth Army. Not only was the German infantry well able to look after itself, if attacked by British tanks, but their anti-tank guns accompanied their tanks and were used boldly, well forward in tank *v* tank engagements.[33] There is little doubt that the belief of British tank crews, that they were being knocked out by German tanks at ranges at which their own guns could not penetrate, originated from this bold use of anti-tank guns. The lack of faith in the 2-pounder spread, in some cases, to the anti-tank artillery accompanying the infantry, and led to the use of 25-pounder field guns as anti-tank artillery (the South Africans had old 18-pounders specifically converted to that rôle). This accentuated the tendency to disperse such field artillery as was available, which was inadequate in quantity in any case, while medium artillery was at a premium. Both the Germans (in Böttcher's Artillery Group 104) and the Italians had an advantage in the heavier calibres. Another cause of the dispersion of artillery was the use of 'columns'. Jock Campbell, who had used them to good effect after *Battleaxe*, was well aware of their limitations. 'They could do any job except two,' he said; 'they could not capture ground from the enemy or deny ground to the enemy.'[34] A balance had to be struck between their contribution in preventing the enemy's reconnaissance units from discovering our dispositions, in misleading him as to our intentions and in harassment, particularly of his supply system, and the need to use all available artillery to support the major action.

A grave handicap was the lack of a suitable vehicle in which infantry could be carried up to the line at which they had to assault the enemy on their feet. The infantry in the German panzer divisions had a number of lightly armoured half-tracked vehicles, although not enough for all. They were not really suitable for use in an assault, although they were so used, certainly in the attack on 5th South African Brigade. The problem of how to employ infantry in the desert, and therefore how to organize it and equip it, was never satisfactorily solved. This thorny problem will be referred to in the context of later operations. At its heart lay the vulnerability of men on their feet, or in unarmoured vehicles, to all forms of fire, particularly artillery and tank fire, and the lack of any natural cover to provide concealment or protection. Auchinleck's conclusion, which was to be reinforced by the events of subsequent months, was that closer co-operation was needed between tanks on the one hand and infantry and artillery on the other, and that a more equal balance between the two elements was needed within the armoured division. To this end, the Support Group of two motor battalions was expanded into a Motor Brigade of three, and every armoured brigade was to be provided, as the 4th had been in *Crusader*, with its own motor batallion and field artillery regiment; but it did not solve the problem of how to use the infantry effectively, especially in the attack.

FOUR

BACK TO GAZALA

In September 1941, in the early days of planning Operation *Crusader*, thought had been given in London as to how to exploit its success. In the hope that it would result in as complete a victory as had O'Connor's at Beda Fomm, Churchill's intention was that it should immediately be followed by Operation *Acrobat*, an advance to Tripoli, while pressure was brought to bear on General Weygand, through the Americans, to invite British forces to join him in French North Africa, the expedition to be known as Operation *Gymnast*. This might be followed by an invasion of Sicily. Since then General Weygand had been dismissed by Vichy, but America's entry into the war had reinforced the case for *Gymnast*, and, as a result of Churchill's visit to confer with Roosevelt in mid-December, the Anglo-American planning for *Gymnast* was put in hand. Churchill was in Washington when *Crusader* came to an end, and immediate pressure was put on Auchinleck to proceed with *Acrobat* with despatch; although, much to the Prime Minister's annoyance, Rommel's forces had not been totally eliminated, Ritchie's logistic situation was precarious, the naval situation in the Mediterranean had taken a turn for the worse, and forces destined for the Middle East had been diverted to the Far East, to which Auchinleck had to contribute also.

The first sign that *Acrobat* was not likely to prove a walk-over was when 22nd Armoured Brigade, the spearhead of Godwin-Austen's follow-up, received a bloody nose on 28 and 29 December near Agedabia from the Afrika Korps, which then had 44 medium and 16 light tanks. For a loss of seven of his own, Crüwell reduced Scott-Cockburn from 90 (55 Crusaders, 35 Stuarts) to 39. Seventh Armoured Division had been replaced by Lumsden's[1] 1st, but Lumsden himself was wounded in an air attack as soon as he arrived in the forward area, and was replaced by Messervy, who had handed over 4th Indian Division to Tuker.[2] Godwin-Austen now had two subordinate formations, 4th Indian Division in the Jebel and 1st Armoured in the desert. The limitations of logistic supply were such that only one brigade of the former, the 7th, commanded by Brigadier H. Briggs,[3] could be kept as far forward as Benghazi; one was with divisional headquarters at Barce, and the other was back at Tobruk – only the 7th was mobile.

Messervy had the tanks of 2nd Armoured Brigade, commanded by Brigadier R. Briggs,[4] in the area between Antelat and Saunnu, attempting to carry out some much-needed training – they had had none since leaving England in September and precious little before that – but were greatly restricted in this by the shortage of petrol. Ninety miles ahead of them, he was keeping contact with Rommel's rearguards which had withdrawn on 6 January 1942 from Agedabia to Mersa Brega. For this purpose the Guards Brigade (renumbered 200 from 22nd) had one battalion forward astride the coast road, forming columns with the whole of its artillery regiment. Its other battalion, with no supporting arms, was 40 miles behind at Agedabia. Some 20 miles south of the Guards' forward columns, 1st Support Group, also with two battalions, was carrying out the same role in difficult country covered in sandy tufts astride the Wadi Faregh. Auchinleck's intention at this time was to resume the offensive as soon as possible in order to turn Rommel out of the El Agheila position. If it were not possible to proceed with *Acrobat*, that would be a much better place at which to stand on the defensive than anywhere further east, which could so easily be outflanked. If that position could not be held, or events on the northern front of his command dictated a withdrawal, his intention, set out in a formal Operation Instruction,[5] was to withdraw all the way to the Egyptian frontier – even further if necessary. The two relevant paragraphs were:

(6) It is not my intention to try and hold permanently Tobruk or any other locality west of the frontier.
(10) Work will be continued in accordance with the original plans on the El Alamein position as opportunity offers, until it is completed.

Messervy's task meanwhile was to harass the enemy while preparations were made for an offensive, and to be ready, if necessary, to fight a defensive battle. He was not happy that his dispositions were suitable for the latter, and proposed that 4th Indian Division should be moved up to Agedabia, with 1st Armoured to the south-east of them; but he was told that transport to maintain so large a force so far forward could only be provided at the expense of the logistic build-up for the resumption of the offensive, which had priority, and which Ritchie hoped to be able to launch in mid-February. In any case nobody at any level expected Rommel to attack before then, as they assumed that he faced logistical problems at least as great, if not greater, than Ritchie's. The staffs at GHQ and Headquarters Eighth Army overestimated the casualties that Rommel had suffered in *Crusader* (although they underestimated his tank losses), and they failed to take account of the supplies delivered to Tripoli since then. On 15 January they estimated his tank strength at 42 German and 40–50 Italian, whereas, on 17 January, it was 84 German and 89 Italian.[6] Auchinleck was repeating the mistake Wavell had made a year before.

Rommel was in fact about to repeat that performance. His staff detected the weakness of Messervy's lay-out, and his wireless intercept service revealed the latter's logistic difficulties. Rommel's intelligence staff pointed out that his own situation would deteriorate as Eighth Army overcame its logistic problems and built up its forces forward of Benghazi. Concealing his intention from his superiors, Rommel struck on 21 January and immediately threw 1st Armoured Division into a state of confusion. By the 23rd, 2nd Armoured Brigade had lost nearly half of its approximately 150 tanks, while 21st Panzer had lost 10 out of its 20 and 15th 19 of its 80.

Godwin-Austen was concerned at the threat to the supply depôt at Msus, where he also had his headquarters. He had no confidence that Messervy could protect it, prevent it being outflanked, and also, if necessary, go to the help of 7th Indian Brigade at Benghazi. He therefore asked Ritchie for permission to withdraw, if necessary, to Mechili. The latter, who had returned on the 22nd to his headquarters at Tmimi from a conference in Cairo about *Acrobat*, and had taken an optimistic view of the situation, calling it 'A God-sent opportunity to hit him really hard when he puts out his neck as it seems possible he is doing',[7] did not refuse it, but urged Godwin-Austen to strengthen his forces both at Benghazi and at Msus, so that he could counter-attack from one of them, if Rommel went for the other. Meanwhile he authorized the precautionary withdrawal of some logistic units and the preparation of demolitions at Benghazi; and the RAF began similar measures, including the abandonment of forward airfields, which were, in any case, seriously waterlogged by recent rain. Rommel, having wasted the 24th looking for 1st Armoured Division, which had moved out of the net he had cast for it, drove north himself on the 25th; he scattered 2nd Armoured Brigade and forced them back in confusion to Msus, where Crüwell stopped, while Briggs took his 41 remaining tanks further north to the edge of the hills at Charruba, 70 miles east of Benghazi. Godwin-Austen now made use of the discretion he had been given, and ordered Tuker to withdraw 7th Brigade from Benghazi and Messervy to take his division 60 miles to the east to Mechili.

Through naval channels Churchill had got to hear of the preparation of demolitions in Benghazi and sent a stinging rebuke by signal to Auchinleck, which brought him and Tedder up to Ritchie's headquarters that afternoon. They persuaded Ritchie to reverse Godwin-Austen's order. Tuker was to order H. Briggs to 'send columns against his [Rommel's] lines of communication northeast of Agedabia', while Messervy opposed any advance towards Charruba and 'protected the left flank of 4th Indian Division'. 'The most offensive action is to be taken, together with greatest risks', were his orders. In a radio conversation Godwin-Austen protested, on the grounds that 1st Armoured Division was not capable of carrying out those tasks; but he was overruled, and Ritchie, on the grounds that his communication with Tuker (which was by line from Tmimi to Barce) was better than Godwin-Austen's, assumed direct command over 4th Indian Division himself. Thereupon Tuker told him that it was impractical for him to do what he had been ordered, with only one brigade forward, which could expect no help from 1st Armoured Division. He was also overruled. After their radio conversation, Godwin-Austen, who had been pressing for a withdrawal to the Gazala line from the 23rd onwards, sent the following signal to Ritchie:

Feel reluctantly compelled to express extreme regret you should persist in altering plans placed before you two days ago and confirmed in your 901 dated 25th Jan. All orders and present movements are based thereon and alterations will cause confusion and lack of confidence in me. Must also protest against alterations having apparently been made at instance of one of my subordinates who made similar proposal to me which I rejected as unsound. I still think so. Though I will do anything to help, you are placing me in very false situation by throwing on me the whole responsibility for ensuring with insufficient means security of force directed by yourself on what I consider an unsound enterprise.[8]

If Auchinleck thought that his appearance at Eighth Army Headquarters was going to have the same effect on events as it appeared to have had in November, he was soon to be disillusioned. Rommel's superiors, Cavallero, Bastico and Kesselring, had visited him on 23 January and attempted to insist that, as there was no immediate prospect of sending him supplies and reinforcement, he should break off his offensive and hold a defensive position at Mersa Brega. Rommel retorted that only Hitler could stop him and that he intended to continue his offensive as long as he could. On 26 January, having detected from wireless intercept that Eighth Army was contemplating withdrawal from Benghazi, and not wishing to leave it in British hands if he made towards Mechili, he decided to use all his motorized infantry to go for the former, while Crüwell's tanks gave the impression that they were heading for the latter. The operation was to start on the 28th. The weather on the intervening days, unfortunately for Ritchie, severely hampered air reconnaissance, and even more unfortunately, one of the few Tac Rs it was possible to carry out spotted the Afrika Korps moving north-east on 27 January. This led Ritchie to assume that Rommel's main thrust was towards Mechili, and he gave orders that night for Messervy next day to attack the rear of the force assumed to be moving east towards Mechili, while Tuker dealt with enemy moving north-west from Msus towards Benghazi. 'The enemy has divided his forces and is weaker than we are in both areas. The keyword is offensive action everywhere.'[9] The effect of these orders was to divide Ritchie's forces even further than they were already, as Messervy moved eastward from Charruba on the 28th.

In fact the forces moving towards Benghazi, which included not only the Marcks Group from Msus, but also 90th Light Division (as Div ZBV had been renamed) and the Italian 20th Corps from the south, were superior to Tuker's 7th Indian Brigade at Benghazi, and by noon, Tuker, reporting their approach, stated that he intended to withdraw unless he could be given the support of the RAF and of 1st Armoured Division. Explaining that the first was difficult, as the RAF had redeployed to the rear, and the second impossible, as they were moving in the opposite direction, Ritchie agreed, and Tuker ordered H. Briggs to execute the demolitions and withdraw during the night. This order came too late, as the Marcks Group, accompanied by Rommel himself, outflanking Benghazi, had cut the main road leading east, and also one north along the coast, by 1800 hrs. Briggs then took the bold decision to drive southwards through the desert in three columns, his 4100 men eventually arriving unharmed at Mechili and El Adem. Rommel entered Benghazi next day, as Eighth Army began its withdrawal, followed up, but not pressed, by the enemy. Ritchie, still trying to counter-attack, wished to hang on to as forward a position as possible, but Tuker emphasized that, without his 7th Brigade, there were more dangers than advantages in trying to stay in the Jebel, and Messervy told Godwin-Austen that he could not deal with more than 25 enemy tanks. Ritchie reluctantly accepted Godwin-Austen's suggestion that he should withdraw to a defensive line at Gazala; and, his advice having been accepted, Godwin-Austen asked to be relieved of his command. With Auchinleck's approval, Ritchie accepted, and Gott was brought up to take over 13th Corps.

Where should the blame for this fiasco lie? Auchinleck, in a letter to his chief of staff, Arthur Smith, and to the Prime Minister, written from Ritchie's headquarters on 30 January,[10] tried to put all the blame on the armour: on its tactical handling by its senior officers; on its failure to co-operate closely with infantry and artillery, and on the inferiority of its equipment, which led to an inferiority complex and loss of morale in its crews. Deficiencies in tactical handling by the totally inexperienced and inadequately trained 2nd Armoured Brigade almost certainly did contribute to tank losses in its engagements with the experienced Afrika Korps, but the unsoundness of the initial layout and the multiplicity of different tasks that the brigade was given in the first few days, which led to different parts of the division being engaged piecemeal, are at least equally to blame. Auchinleck must bear the blame for placing Ritchie, Godwin-Austen and their subordinates in a fundamentally unsound position. If Messervy's proposal to concentrate 4th Indian and 1st Armoured Divisions at Agedabia had been accepted, Rommel would probably never have chanced his arm. If that was not possible for logistic reasons, a closer concentration of the two divisions near Benghazi would have been preferable to the wide dispersion adopted. Messervy and Raymond Briggs cannot be blamed for failure to co-ordinate armour and other arms, when their orders forced infantry and armour so far apart.

As to subsequent events, there can be little doubt, with the advantage of hindsight, that Godwin-Austen's realistic advice was preferable to the airy optimism pressed on Ritchie by Auchinleck, breathing down his neck for the whole week from 25 January to 1 February. Behind that, of course, was the hot breath of Churchill, whose pressure for *Acrobat* was the real problem. On 28 January the Prime Minister had signalled:

You have no doubt seen most secret stuff about Rommel's presumed intentions namely clearing up triangle Benghazi-Msus-Mechili and then withdrawing to waiting line about Agheila. This seems to reinforce importance of our holding on.[11]

Nevertheless, it was not unreasonable to assume that Rommel could not sustain a major offensive, when the strength of his forces was so low and his logistic supply so precarious. His own superiors took this view. Nor was it unreasonable to expect that a force of the strength of Messervy's division should have been able to inflict sufficient loss on one such as Rommel initially deployed, to have made Rommel's capture of Benghazi impossible. But numbers alone do not dictate results on the battlefield, as subsequent events were to show.

There are those who maintain that, instead of accepting Godwin-Austen's resignation, Auchinleck should have removed Ritchie,[12] perhaps replacing him with Godwin-Austen. While he may have sympathized with the latter, it is clear that it would have been almost impossible for Auchinleck to have made the change, when Ritchie had been so loyally passing on the orders dictated by Auchinleck himself. He would have been using Ritchie as a scapegoat for himself, as he was to do indirectly after the war.

Before Gott arrived on 5 February to take over 13th Corps on the Gazala line, Auchinleck, back in Cairo, after consultation with his fellow Commanders-in-Chief, sent Ritchie new orders. His tasks were:

(a) To hold the enemy as far west of Tobruk as possible without risking defeat in detail;

(b) To organize a striking-force with which to resume the offensive, with the object of destroying the enemy forces in the field, and occupying Cyrenaica at the earliest possible date;

(c) To study the possibility of regaining the landing-grounds in the area Derna-Martuba-Mechili for our air forces at an early date, provided this can be done without prejudice to the tasks defined at (a) and (b).

(d) To prevent to the utmost extent possible, without prejudice to the tasks defined in (a) and (b), the use by the enemy force of the landing-grounds in the area of Derna-Martuba-Mechili;

(e) To avoid your forces being invested in Tobruk in the event of our having to withdraw to the east of that place;

(f) To complete the preparation of defensive positions on the general line Sollum-Maddalena-Jiarabub at the earliest possible date.[13]

The last two tasks certainly implied that, if the Gazala line could not be held, the next step back would be the Sollum-Maddalena line; according to Gott's Brigadier General Staff, Erskine,[14] the possibility of the latter was very much in Gott's mind when he assumed command, and for some time after. But, as Eighth Army's strength was built up and the logistic preparations for a future offensive gained momentum, including the extension of the railway from Misheifa, south of Sollum, to No. 4 Forward Base at Belhamed outside Tobruk, consideration of a fall-back to the frontier was superseded by emphasis on preparations for the future offensive.

The date on which such an offensive could be launched was the subject of an increasingly acrimonious exchange of signals between Cairo and London. Churchill, anxious about the critical situation of Malta, less and less able both to exist without supplies and to provide a base for interference with those of Rommel's Panzerarmee, pressed for the earliest possible date, pointing out that Rommel would benefit as much as Ritchie, if not more from delay. Auchinleck, supported by his fellow Commanders-in-Chief, insisted that it could not be launched until Ritchie had a 3:2 advantage in numbers of tanks over Rommel – preferably three armoured divisions. This would not be the case until June. Churchill and the Chiefs of Staff pressed for a much earlier date, so that the airfields of Cyrenaica could be used to escort a convoy to Malta from Alexandria in the moonless period of April. In mid-May they were still arguing about the date on which Ritchie would launch Operation *Buckshot*.

Ritchie was determined not to become embroiled in a methodical slow advance through the difficult country of the Gebel. He wished to turn the tables on Rommel and cut him off in turn. The general plan was for 13 Corps to contain Rommel's force frontally, while Norrie's 30 Corps would advance over the good 'going' due west from Bir Hacheim, 50 miles south-west of

Tobruk. Every 30 miles, an infantry brigade group would be established in a defensive box. If Rommel reacted, he would have to move his panzer divisions southwards, well away from the static Italian divisions, and would be engaged by Norrie's armoured divisions operating between these boxes. If he did not react and preferred to concentrate against Gott, Norrie would cut him off from his supplies by establishing his armoured divisions on the old battlegrounds of Msus and Sceleidima, threatening Benghazi itself. It was an ambitious plan, and many, including Gott and Norrie, thought it impracticable. The important point is that the demands of the plan, combined with the desire to keep Rommel at a long arm's distance from the forward base, drew the southern end of Eighth Army's defence line well down to the south-west of Tobruk.[15]

However, from 13 May onwards, it became increasingly clear that Rommel was intending to launch a major attack, and Ritchie obtained Auchinleck's permission to give defence priority over preparing *Buckshot*.

FIVE

GAZALA — THE FIRST PHASE

The battles which followed, known as the Battle of Gazala, led to the total defeat of Eighth Army, the loss of Tobruk and the retreat to El Alamein. Nobody involved has escaped criticism for all that went wrong, but most of it has been concentrated on Ritchie. The burden of it has been that Ritchie should not have been appointed to command Eighth Army in the first place, lacking experience of command and of active operations in the desert; that, both in the *Crusader* operation and in the Gazala battles of June 1942, he was over-optimistic in his assessment of the situation and in his reports to Auchinleck; that the layout of Eighth Army round Tobruk, when Rommel attacked on 27 May, was unsound, notably in the disposition of the armour, over which Ritchie disregarded Auchinleck's advice, which was sounder; that the various plans for counter-attacking Rommel, in what was called the Cauldron, were ill-conceived and badly planned and executed; that Ritchie should not have given Koenig's Free French Brigade permission to withdraw from Bir Hacheim when he did; that he both deceived Auchinleck and disobeyed his orders in ordering the withdrawal of 1st South African and 50th Divisions from the Gazala defences on 14 June, after the disastrous defeat of the armour on the previous day; and that he committed the same offences in his reaction to Auchinleck's order to hold Rommel on the line of Acroma-El Adem-Bir Gubi thereafter.

The impression is often given that it was the initial layout of Eighth Army that was at fault, and that this dictated all that followed. It is generally true to say that, although everything was by no means lost on the first day of the Gazala battles (27 May 1942), Eighth Army never really recovered from the confusion into which it was thrown on that day. However, Rommel's Panzerarmee Afrika was also thrown into considerable confusion on that day, as his account in *The Rommel Papers*[1] makes vividly clear.

The events of 27 May therefore call for detailed examination. Map 5 shows the dispositions of Eighth Army on 26 May, and its intelligence estimate of Rommel's dispositions at the same time. Correlli Barnett made a general

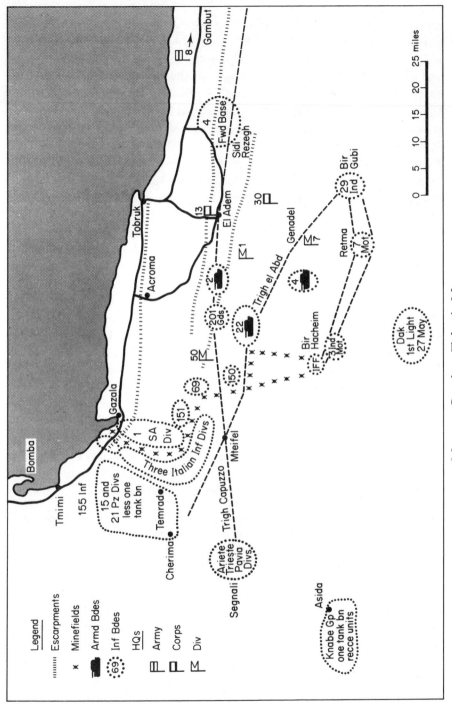

Map 5   Gazala – Tobruk, May 1942

criticism of the layout, suggesting that Ritchie should have held no fixed positions, but kept his army as O'Connor had in the winter of 1940, 'sixty miles behind the lines of his forward patrols, protected thereby from surprise and sudden shock'.[2] This naïve comment totally disregarded the fact that, up to 13 May, Ritchie was supposed to be planning an *offensive* to recapture Cyrenaica in order that the RAF, from airfields in 'The Bulge', could give air cover to a convoy sailing from Alexandria to the relief of beleaguered Malta. If Ritchie had kept his main forces 60 miles behind his forward patrols, Rommel would have walked into Tobruk. His Panzerarmee could not be relied upon to remain inactive, like Berti's Tenth Italian Army at Sidi Barrani in 1940. Eighth Army's general layout was designed to keep Rommel away from Tobruk, to the immediate south-east of which a vast forward base was built up, supplied by rail and pipeline, as well as through Tobruk by sea. The purpose of the base was to support the future offensive, which Auchinleck was being urgently pressed by Churchill and the Chiefs of Staff to undertake at the earliest possible moment.

The principal accusation, from many sources, is that Ritchie's armour was too greatly dispersed, and that at least the three armoured brigades in the two armoured divisions, 1st and 7th, under Norrie's 30th Corps, should, as Auchinleck suggested to Ritchie in a letter on 20 May, quoted in full by Connell,[3] be concentrated further north astride the Trigh Capuzzo. This letter is vital to the whole controversy, and all parts of it must be taken into account. Auchinleck stated that there were two courses of action open to the enemy: either to envelop Eighth Army's southern flank, seizing or masking Bir Hacheim en route, and then driving on to Tobruk, accompanied by a strong diversion in the north, and possibly landings from the sea near Gazala; or to put in a very heavy attack on a narrow front against the centre of the main position, with the object of driving straight to Tobruk.

This would probably be helped by a feint against Bir Hacheim, in which the Italian tanks might well be used with the aim of drawing off the main body of your armour to the south, and so leaving the way open for the main thrust. This course would also almost certainly include an attack from the sea round about Gazala.

He stressed that he believed Rommel would adopt the second course, which was the most dangerous to Eighth Army, and went into considerable detail of how he thought Rommel would carry out his attack, which he expected would establish a narrow corridor on the boundary between 1st South African and 50th Divisions. In the light of his assumption, he suggested that Ritchie should place his 'armoured reserve a good deal further to the north where it can hit the enemy immediately he emerges from his breakthrough,

1 Generals Wavell (right) and O'Connor

2 Bren-gun carriers passing Fort Capuzzo after its capture in June 1940

3 Rolls-Royce armoured car of the 11th Hussars, 1940–1

4 Matilda tank of the 7th Royal Tank Regiment at a captured Italian gun position at Sidi Barrani, December 1940

5 Sollum Bay, looking towards the foot of Halfaya Pass

6 Light-tank crew brewing up, winter 1940–1

7 Infantry of 6th Australian Division attacking Bardia, 3 January 1941

8 The desert – a typical day

9 Crusader tanks

10   Two-pounder portée
anti-tank gun

12   (Opposite) General Crüwell,
commander of the Afrika Korps,
and Colonel Bayerlein, his chief
of staff

11   (Below) Rommel and
staff-officers of the Afrika Korps

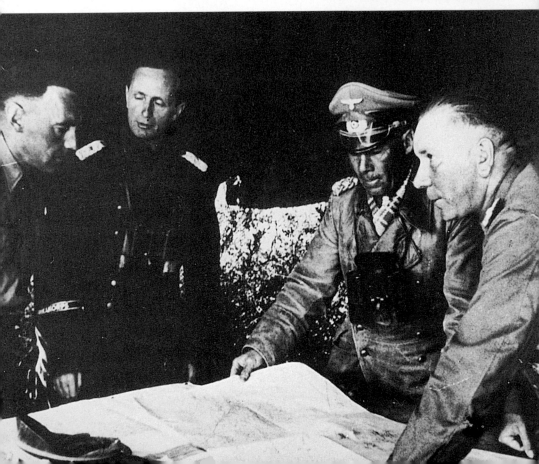

13 General von Ravenstein, commander of 21st Panzer Division, after his capture on 29 November 1941

14 General Neumann-Silkow

15   Rommel with the Italian Generals Bastico and Cavallero

16   General Gambara

17 Air Vice Marshal Coningham, commander of the Desert Air Force, HRH The Duke of Gloucester, and General Ritchie, May 1942

18 General Cunningham in Operation Crusader, November 1941

19 Major-General Morshead, commander of 9th Australian Division, HRH The Duke of Gloucester, and General Wilson, May 1942

20 Matilda tank crew, carrying out maintenance

21 American M3 light Stuart
tank, known as the 'Honey',
with which 4th Armoured
Brigade was equipped in
Operation *Crusader* – November
1941

22 (Opposite top)
Twenty-five-pounder field gun

23 (Opposite bottom) The
dreaded German 88mm anti-tank
gun, and its half-tracked tractor.
It was designed as an
anti-aircraft gun

24 German half-tracked
personnel carrier–it was not
armoured

25 Infantry in the desert in
winter. This rocky ground is
typical of that found on the edge
of escarpments. It was
impossible to dig into

26 German anti-tank mines. They would break a track or blow in the belly-plate of a tank

27 German Mark II Light tank. Equipped with a 20mm heavy machine gun, it carried no anti-tank weapon

28 German Mark IIIH Medium tank with short 50mm gun, carrying tracks over the front plate to provide extra protection

29 German Mark IIIJ Medium tank with the long 50mm gun, a very effective anti-tank weapon

30 German Mark IV Medium tank with the short 75mm gun, designed to fire high-explosive shell

31 Burning German truck, probably after being blown up by the sappers

32 General Ritchie (centre), with his corps commanders, Generals Norrie (left) and Gott, May/June 1942

33 General Messervy (left) when commanding 4th Indian Division, December 1941

34 Lieut-Colonel Hartnell, commander of the 19th New Zealand Infantry Battalion and Brigadier Willison, commander 32nd Army Tank Brigade, at their link-up at Ed Duda, 27 November 1941

35 The American Grant tank, first used by British armoured regiments of 1st and 7th Armoured Divisions in May 1942. Note the 37mm gun in the turret and the 75mm in the sponson

36 (Opposite top) Valentine tanks, the front one without a gun, perhaps used as a command tank

37 (Opposite bottom) The British 6-pounder anti-tank gun, first used in May 1942

38 (Opposite top) German
50mm anti-tank gun, one of the
most effective weapons in the
desert

39 (Opposite bottom) German
Mark IV Special Medium tank.
It first appeared in the desert, in
small numbers, in May 1942

40 (right) General Ramsden
(left), commander of 50th
Division May-June 1942 and
30th Corps July 1942

41 (below) Left to right:
Generals R. Briggs, Freyberg,
Gatehouse, Lumsden and
Gairdner before the Battle of El
Alamein

42 Generals Montgomery (second left), Leese (second right) and Lumsden (right) with Lieutenant-Colonel Douglas Darling

and before he can establish a defensive flank'; that 'both armoured divisions complete should be positioned astride the Trigh Capuzzo', and added:

It does not look from the map as if this would be too far north to meet the main attack should it come round the southern flank, instead of against the centre as I anticipate. Your covering troops should give you good warning of any main enveloping movement on your left, even if you do not hear of it before it starts. As always, the difficulty will be to decide which is the real attack and which the feint.

Auchinleck appreciated that Ritchie's reaction to his suggestion to move 7th Armoured Division north to join the 1st, which was already deployed in the area he suggested, would be that Eighth Army's southern flank would be left bare of any mobile troops to delay and harass the enemy, and also of any armoured units to give immediate support to the Free French; he therefore proposed to send up 3rd Indian Motor Brigade, which 'although not absolutely fully equipped, is fit for battle'. This would obviate any need to leave either of the motor brigades of the two armoured divisions in this area 'so that they could fight as divisions'. (In fact, only one battalion and two field artillery batteries of 7th Armoured Division's motor brigade were so employed.) He would also send up an additional battalion of 'Infantry' tanks and an additional armoured brigade for 7th Armoured Division (neither of them arrived before Rommel attacked). He suggested that all the 'I' tanks of 1st and 32nd Army Tank Brigades should 'be placed to support the infantry in that part of the position which is likely to bear the brunt of the enemy attack' to 'encourage the infantry to hang on'. He suggested that Ritchie should lay more mines both in the rear of 13th Corps's positions 'and cover these with guns' and thicken up minefields in the 'coastal corridor'. Another Indian infantry brigade would be sent up, so that Ritchie could use one of the brigades of 5th Indian Division to 'fortify El Gubi and protect it with mines', which he imagined would 'threaten any wide turning moment from the south against Tobruk or from the west against Sollum', as if an infantry brigade, dug into a defensive position in the desert, could threaten anything beyond the range of its guns. Finally he suggested that all the static positions, all the way from Gazala to Bir Gubi, should be under command of Gott's 13th Corps, while Norrie's task should be limited to 'hitting the enemy wherever he may thrust, and destroy him'.

This letter was brought to Ritchie by Auchinleck's chief of staff, Corbett,[4] to whom Ritchie explained the plan that he had agreed with Norrie. Thirtieth Corps war diary[5] includes 30 Corps Operation Instruction 42 of 20 May, which shows clearly what that was:

12. *Plan A*

If enemy's main attack is directed along the coast and between the coast and northern escarpment (i.e. the one immediately south of the coast road);

1 Armd Div will NOT go NORTH of the northern escarpment but will

(i) Secure the routes over the southern-escarpment north and NW of EL ADEM leading towards TOBRUCH

(ii) Be prepared to destroy the enemy debouching SOUTH on either side of ACROMA.

(b) 7 Armd Div will remain responsible for the protection of the left flank between incl BIR HACHEIM and BIR GUBI. 7 Armd Div will NOT commit 4 Armd Bde without reference to 30 Corps.

13. *Plan B*

If the enemy makes his main attack through our minefields either astride the TRIGH CAPUZZO or SOUTH of it;

(a) 1 Armd Div will destroy the enemy before he reaches the line ACROMA – EL ADEM;

(b) 7 Armd Div as in 12(b) above.

14. *Plan C*

If the enemy attack in force SOUTH of BIR HACHEIM;

(a) 7 Armd Div will delay the enemy in order that he may be destroyed if possible by all our armour on general line of southern track BIR HACHEIM – BIR GUBI;

(b) 1 Armd Div will be prepared to move SOUTH to engage the enemy either:

(i) On general line of southern track BIR HACHEIM – BIR GUBI on LEFT of 7 Armd Div

or (ii) on general line of TRIGH EL ABD probably on RIGHT of 7 Armd Div who will be about GENADEL.

(iii) The move SOUTH to support 7 Armd Div may be by whole 1 Armd Div, but probably 201 Gds Bde and possibly one armd bde may have to remain in the northern area.

These paragraphs were followed by one on 'Liaison', which provided for 1st Armoured Division to listen to the regimental frequencies of the armoured car regiments under command of 7th Armoured Division and to provide liaison officers with wireless sets at Headquarters 50th Division and with 8th Royal Tanks (Valentine tanks north of them) and for 7th Armoured Division to ensure that 50th Division knew the frequencies of the armoured car regiments operating south of them (4th South African Armoured Car Regiment), and that direct communication was established between the Free French Brigade at Bir Hacheim and Headquarters 30 Corps, when the enemy advanced.

The accusation has been made that Ritchie deceived Auchinleck as to the positioning and plans for the armour; or that, at least, there was a genuine misunderstanding, Auchinleck believing that Ritchie had accepted his advice and the latter that Auchinleck was satisfied that his plan met Auchinleck's points. In particular Ritchie agreed that 7th Armoured Division should be relieved of its left flank protection rôle, including command of the armoured car screen, which was maintaining contact with the enemy west of the minefields; of 3rd Indian Motor Brigade, which would relieve 7th Motor Brigade of the task of supporting them; and of the static positions of 1st Free French Brigade at Bir Hacheim and 29th Indian Infantry Brigade at Bir Gubi. This would be effected as soon as Major General Tuker, with the operational element of 4th Indian Division Headquarters, could be made available for this task. Ritchie had not accepted, for good practical reasons, that Tuker, when he arrived, would come under command of Gott. He had not done so when Rommel attacked. There is no evidence that Ritchie deceived Auchinleck, nor that there was any misunderstanding. If there was, the blame must be attributed to Corbett.

In a letter to Auchinleck on 23 May, Ritchie expressed his doubt about the latter's forecast that the main attack would come in the centre. He pointed out that improvements in Rommel's logistic situation would

give him a great circuit of action for his striking force. I still feel that if his maintenance makes this possible he will try to go round our southern flank. In any case there will be a diversion there and it will probably be the Italian Mobile Corps (Ariete armoured and Trieste motorized divisions). There are certainly indications of an interest on his part in the BREGHISC—ALEM HAMZA ridge [the area suggested by Auchinleck] and the main thrust may, of course, come here. But it will be a difficult and costly operation for him as our minefields are strong and our positions there well sited, well supported with artillery and well dug-in. Anyhow whatever course he may adopt, our main strength is the counter with our armour to destroy him. We are ready for this ... the ground carefully studied, and I feel confident that our armed [?armoured] forces are prepared to operate either to the south or to the north-west.

Ritchie had come to this conclusion in an appreciation written on 13 May and forwarded personally to Norrie and Gott on 17 May.[7]

This letter crossed one of the same date from Auchinleck, in which the latter wrote: 'I am quite happy about the positioning of the armoured divisions, and I am glad that we were thinking on the same lines.'[8] Ritchie wrote again on the 25th, saying: 'I am so pleased to feel that you are happy about the positioning of the armour. I was sure you would be once you were in possession of the correct facts,' to which Auchinleck replied next day, arguing against Ritchie's fears for his southern flank:

I have never discarded the possibility of the enemy making his main thrust round the southern flank, and it would be dangerous to make up one's mind that he must attack in one place only. Nevertheless, my opinion, for what it is worth, is that the great majority of the indications point to a very heavy attack on a narrow front on the northern sector of your front, probably against the front of the 1st South African Brigade [the southernmost brigade of 1st South African Division].

Having made some suggestions for altering its dispositions (which would have involved giving up the commanding high ground), he wrote:

If he comes by the south, time should be on your side, and you ought to get ample warning from your motorized troops, armoured cars and the air. An offensive on this flank will very soon expose his supply lines to your attack, and should give you the chance of having at his weak infantry, once he has committed his armour beyond Bir Hacheim. Do you agree with this?[9]

By the time Ritchie received this letter, Rommel had launched Operation *Venezia*.

We must now consider what Ritchie's 'armoured reserve' consisted of and how it compared with the tank strength of Rommel's Panzerarmee. The slow infantry support or 'I' tanks in 1st and 32nd Army Tank Brigades were under command of 13th Corps and not regarded as part of the armoured reserve. First Army Tank Brigade had two regiments of Matildas: one of them, with one squadron from the other, was with 50th Division and the other with 1st South African. Its third regiment, 8th Royal Tanks, of Valentines, was split between two mobile columns operating under command of 2nd South African Division west of the defences of Tobruk, south of Acroma. Thirty-second Army Tank Brigade, with one regiment each of Matildas and Valentines, arrived just as the battle started, the Matildas reinforcing 1st South African Division and the Valentines joining 7th Armoured Division after Rommel had attacked, bringing the total of 'I' tanks to 110 Matildas and 167 Valentines. In 30th Corps Norrie had 573 tanks – 167 Grants, 149 Stuarts and 257 Crusaders, the six armoured regiments of 1st Armoured Division's two armoured brigades, 2nd and 22nd, each having one squadron of Grants and two of Crusaders, while the three regiments of 7th Armoured Division's 4th Armoured Brigade each had two squadrons of Grants and one of Stuarts. In Rommel's Panzerarmee, the two panzer divisions of the Afrika Korps, 15th and 21st, had a total of 332 German tanks and the Italian XX Mobile Corps 228 Italian M13s. Ritchie's 850 tanks against Rommel's 560 therefore gave him the 3:2 superiority on which Auchinleck had insisted before he could launch an offensive.

The significant changes in the quality on both sides, as compared with that which obtained in *Crusader*, were the introduction in Eighth Army of the Grant tanks and the 6-pounder anti-tank gun; and, in Rommel's panzer divisions, the up-armouring of all the Mark IIIHs, which still carried the old short 50mm gun, and the introduction of small numbers of the Mark IIIJ, which had the same long 50mm as the anti-tank gun, and of the Mark IV (Special) with a long, high velocity 75mm gun; but on 27 May they had only 19 Mark IIIJs and 4 Mark IV Specials. The Grant tank had a 37mm gun, the same as in the Stuart, in its turret, and a 75mm of moderate velocity in a sponson in the hull. The 75mm could penetrate the thickened front plate of the Mark IIIH and those of the Mark IIIJ and the Mark IV, probably at 850 and certainly at 650 yards range, while its own frontal armour was proof against the long 50mm at 1000 yards and against the short 50mm even at 250 yards. All of the 112 6-pounder anti-tank guns were allotted to 30th Corps and were distributed to the motor brigades of the two armoured divisions.

Whatever method of comparison is used, there is no doubt that, on a purely technical basis, Norrie's 573 should have been able to defeat Rommel's 447 medium tanks (the others were light tanks or command vehicles), and that 4th Armoured Brigade on its own should have been able to defeat either panzer division. If joined by either 2nd or 22nd Armoured Brigade, it should have been able to defeat the whole Afrika Korps. If the latter had already had to force its way through the positions of 13th Corps, supported by the 'I' tanks, it could be assumed that it would have suffered significant tank casualties before meeting the armoured brigades of 1st Armoured Division, which should then have been able to defeat it. Ritchie was therefore entirely justified in assuming that Norrie's initial dispositions provided sufficient tank strength to secure him against a breakthrough to Tobruk in the centre. If Rommel came round the south, not only would the Italian Mobile Corps probably be involved as well as the Afrika Korps, but neither would have had to fight their way through any defences which might take toll of them, unless they chose, at Bir Hacheim, to attack the French, whom they could easily by-pass. If 7th Armoured Division were moved further north, Rommel might have a clear run to the area east of El Adem, which included the vast No. 4 Forward Base, built up to support the offensive, which had only been temporarily postponed, and about which Auchinleck was still arguing with Churchill. If Rommel reached the base, he could afford to forget his 'vulnerable supply line', except for ammunition; would throw the whole of Eighth Army's command and logistic organization into confusion, and would threaten the forward airfields round Gambut. It must be realized that the area behind the combat troops was littered with unit and formation transport, repair and other logistic units, as well as headquarters. Ritchie was therefore rightly reluctant to run risks on his southern flank for the sake of over-insuring against Auchinleck's forecast of an attack in the centre. In a move round the south, Rommel's tanks, from where they were thought to be, would have to travel 65 miles to reach the area in which it was planned that 7th Armoured Division would engage such a threat (55 miles from where they actually were on 26 May). The time it would take them to do this, which would involve refuelling, should be ample to enable either or both of 1st Armoured Division's armoured brigades (22nd 12 and 2nd 15 miles) to be moved to join the 4th. In the event it took Rommel 13 hours. The mistake that everybody made, including Auchinleck, Ritchie, Norrie and Messervy, was to assume both that they would have accurate information of Rommel's moves and that the combination of armoured cars, motorized infantry and two batteries of 25-pounder field guns could impose significant delay on a force of several hundred tanks. Insufficient attention seems to have been paid to what the situation would be if Rommel chose to move by night, as he did, in spite of the fact that he had been surprised in the previous November by an almost identical night approach march at the start of Operation *Crusader*. Thirty Corps Operation Order No. 42, already quoted, and Operation Instruction No. 46 of 26 May,[10] to which further reference will be made, envisaged a phase of 'closing-up' to our minefields before the main attack was launched.

Why did Ritchie's plan fail? The answer lies partly in what was in the minds of the principal commanders concerned in 30th Corps, and partly in what actually happened on 26 and 27 May. Important records concerning both are either missing altogether or very inadequate. The main gaps lie in the lack of any record of most of the important telephone conversations between the commanders, or of verbal exchanges when they met, and in the fact that important war diaries were written up after the event, the actual signal log having been either not kept or destroyed to avoid capture by the enemy. However, some important operation orders and intelligence summaries have survived, as have the signal logs of the operational command vehicles of Main Headquarters 30th Corps and Tactical and Main Headquarters Eighth Army.

The minds of all the commanders of 30th Corps were affected by the correlation between the advice of the Commander-in-Chief (which Ritchie loyally passed on, although he did not agree with significant aspects of it) and the assessment of the intelligence staffs (which, no doubt, influenced Auchinleck's guesswork). Professor Hinsley has dealt with the latter in some detail in Volume II of his *Official History of British Intelligence in the Second World War*.[11] ULTRA gave clear warning that Rommel was intending an offensive and that his attack could be expected at any time after 22 May, but gave no indication as to the form it would take. For clues to that Eighth Army relied principally on photographic air reconnaissance of changes in his dispositions and on 'Y', the tactical army wireless intercept service. It was unfortunate that less attention was paid to the latter than to the former. There is not the space, nor is there the need, to go into detail here. The intelligence picture of Rommel's dispositions on 26 May, before he began his advance, is that shown in Map 5. The principal uncertainty concerned the dispositions of 90th Light Division, the motorized infantry division of the Afrika Korps, from which a prisoner had been captured by one of 7th Armoured Division's armoured car patrols on 23 May. His evidence, that his division and a large number of tanks – probably 21st Panzer Division – were at Asida, was not surprisingly disbelieved.

The clearest clue to Norrie's thoughts is given by 30 Corps Operation Instruction No. 46. This was a personal instruction from him to Major Generals Lumsden, Messervy and Tuker, signed by his Brigadier General Staff, G. S. Hatton, at 2305 hrs on 26 May and delivered by liaison officer to its addressees. It was probably dictated by Norrie to his excellent personal assistant, a Sergeant Clerk in the RASC, in the late afternoon of that day, and its intelligence assessment was clearly based on Eighth Army Intelligence Summary No. 216, based on information available there from 0800 hrs 25 to 0800 hrs 26 May.[12] That summary had concluded that 'the main German armour is in the Northern sector', that '132 ARIETE division is still in the SEGNALI sector', and that 'There are about 30 tanks in the area EL ASIDA'.

Norrie's instruction is of critical importance and is worth quoting at length:

Evidence from most sources indicates that the enemy's preparations for an offensive are nearing completion, although in point of fact there has been little collaboration [sic] until this afternoon as far as observation by forward troops is concerned. The enemy is still some way from contact with our northerly positions, and no reconnaissances of our minefields have taken place except from the air. As usual, the enemy appears to be preceding his main attack by a 'recce in force' including tanks. This was developing today on a medium scale EAST of SEGNALI, where our armoured car screen has been pushed back 7/15 miles. Apart from some shelling in the NORTH and some Stuka dive-bombing on 26 May, the enemy ground forces have until today shown little interest in our positions. 13 Corps destroyed 9 Stukas and 2 German tanks today.

This was followed by a paragraph about possible parachute and amphibious landings, the former estimated at a maximum of 600 paratroops from Crete and the latter at 2000 men.

Having said that the enemy dispositions appeared to be as shown on Map 5, he continued:

Conclusion. From the foregoing, it still appears probable that the main weight of the enemy offensive will be in the NORTH, but at the same time a thrust SOUTH of BIR HACHEIM becomes more of a threat than a diversion. It may be that ARIETE will be dispatched to attack our troops in the SOUTH, with the objective of EL ADEM, while the Battle Group KNABE proceeds eastwards under cover of ARIETE's attack, turning NORTH or NW at a favourable opportunity.

A possible objective for the KNABE Gp might be our railhead area at CAPUZZO, in conjunction with sea or airborne landings, or a combination of both. The latter is a course which I consider unlikely, but at the same time it must not be dismissed as impossible.

I consider, on all the evidence in our possession, that the enemy is almost certain to make an attack in the immediate future. In terms of betting, I regard the chances of such an offensive starting before 31 May as 4 to 1 ON. Such an attack is likely to be preceded by parachute or seaborne landings in our administrative areas. The enemy is likely to thrust both in the NORTH and SOUTH and to exploit success as best he can, to secure his main objective TOBRUK. It would seem that an attack against 13 Corps is the more likely course, with a thrust round our SOUTH flank.

There is, however, at present insufficient data to forecast with exactitude where his main thrusts will be launched, so we must be prepared, as we are, to meet an attack on both Corps fronts.

INTENTION.

13. My intention remains the same as stated in Op Inst. No 42 of 20 May, namely, in cooperation with 13 Corps, to destroy the enemy's armoured forces in the battle for the position GAZALA-TOBRUCH-HACHEIM, as the initial step in securing CYRENAICA.

30 Corps roles remain the same with the addition that, in any counter-offensive after the enemy attack has been broken, 30 Corps will be prepared to capture MECHILI.

Two paragraphs about the counter-offensive followed, and then:

Provision must be made for the future, but the most urgent matter is to win the main battle first. Once accomplished, the fruits of victory must not be allowed to escape us.

14. *Role of 1 Armd Div.* Same as given in Op Inst No 42.

15. *Role of 7 Armd Div.* 7 Armd Div will continue to observe and harass the enemy on the Corps front until relieved of this task by 4 Ind Div. Comd 7 Armd Div will report the earliest date by which he considers it possible to relieve 7 Mot Bde by 3 Ind Mot Bde. 7 Armd Div will continue with the arrangements already made for a coln from 3 Ind Mot Bde to observe the minefields between BIR HACHEIM and 50 Div on the eastern side.

16. It will not be easy in the opening stages to know for certain where the enemy thrust is being launched. The enemy may well attack at several points and exploit where he considers success most probable, and do all he can to deceive us of his real intentions.

17.(a) If the enemy directs a heavy attack through our minefields on or NORTH of the TRIGH CAPUZZO area, 7 Armd Div will make every effort to delay and contain any enemy forces operating against our southern flank. Early information of the size, identity and direction of such an advance should be obtained from armoured car patrols and delay imposed by columns. Under these circumstances, 4 Armd Bde will NOT be employed and in the initial stages of the battle will be considered as in Corps reserve. If the enemy armour is considered to be of such a size as to warrant the employment of 4 Armd Bde, Comd 7 Armd Div will report the fact immediately for my decision and will prevent the enemy moving NORTH of the line BIR HACHEIM-BIR EL GUBI or EAST of the Wadi es SCIAABA [which ran more or less due south from BIR GUBI].

If 4 Armd Bde has to be employed EAST of our minefields and NORTH of a general line BIR EL HARMAT – B367 – BIR EL HAIAD [a line drawn from where 22 Armd Bde to where HQ 30 Corps are shown on Map 5], it will come either directly under comd 30 Corps or under comd 1 Armd Div. As such a transfer is only likely to be of very temporary character, it is intended that 4 Armd Bde should remain under 7 Armd Div for adm(inistration) in either eventuality.

(b) If the enemy's main attack is directed SOUTH of BIR HACHEIM, 7 Armd Div will hold the enemy and destroy him on the general line BIR HACHEIM- BIR EL GUBI. 1 Armd Div, or part of it, will be prepared to cooperate according to the demands of the situation as a whole in accordance with orders issued by 30 Corps.

(c) On arrival of Operational HQ 4 Ind Div, 7 Armd Div will hand over comd of 29 Ind Inf Bde to them. When HQ 3 Ind Mot Bde have relieved HQ 7 Mot Bde, 7 Armd Div will hand over comd of following tps to 4 Ind Div:

> 3 Ind Mot Bde
> 1 FF Bde
> KDG or 13 L, if latter have
> > relieved KDG
>
> 4 SAAC
> One sqn 4 R Tanks.

7 Armd Div will then come into Corps reserve.

(d) If the enemy attack fails, wherever it may be directed, 7 Armd Div will be prepared to advance immediately with the object of capturing MECHILI.

WARNING. It is impossible to lay down how much warning formations may get before they are ordered to move. In order to allow vehicles to be repaired in unit lines and for training in new equipment, formations are placed at four hours notice to move. [They had actually been at that notice since 25 May.] Comds must however ensure that there are NOT either so many vehicles under repair nor so many troops training away from their concentration areas that units cannot operate immediately if ordered to do so.

There is no record of the time when the liaison officers delivered the instruction to Headquarters 1st and 7th Armoured Divisions, nor of whether Lumsden and Messervy had been woken up to read it. Before considering the actual events of that crucial night, we must look at such evidence as exists of what their thoughts were before it was brought to their headquarters.

First, Lumsden's 1st Armoured Division. As it was the area which concerned him most, Lumsden was naturally inclined to regard an attack on the centre as the one to which he should give priority. His division's Operation Order No. 15 of 20 May[13] discussed the three choices open to Rommel – along the coast, astride the Trigh Capuzzo, and round south of Bir Hacheim – and concluded:

We may therefore expect a preliminary attack on the whole of our defensive system, coupled with an attempt to outflank HACHEIM. The main weight of the enemy attack is most likely to develop astride the TRIGH CAPUZZO and via the gap north of HACHEIM, as it is in these areas that we are less strong and an initial success is most likely to be achieved by the enemy.

The action to be taken was divided into two phases, the first while the enemy closed up to our positions, the second 'when the enemy's main thrust has been disclosed'. The plan followed that laid down in 30 Corps Operation Order No. 42 and stated that, if the enemy main thrust came south of Bir Hacheim, and the division moved either to the left of 7th Armoured Division on the Hacheim – Gubi track, or to its right on the Trigh El Abd,

it is possible that Guards Brigade and 22nd Armoured Brigade will remain in positions arranged for them. In this event 2nd Armoured Brigade Group alone will cooperate with 7th Armoured Division for the destruction of the enemy when have moved (sic) SOUTH of BIR HACHEIM.

There was another factor affecting Lumsden's state of mind, which is not recorded, but of which I was very much aware, and which made him very reluctant to agree to either of his armoured brigades being transferred to the command of 7th Armoured Division at any time. Twenty-second Armoured Brigade had been sent out to the Middle East ahead of the rest of the division and had joined 7th Armoured Division for the *Crusader* operation in November 1941, in which it had suffered significant casualties. As has been related, very shortly after the rest of the division had arrived and relieved 7th Armoured Division in the forward area south of Benghazi in January 1942, regaining command of 22nd Armoured Brigade, Lumsden was wounded in an air attack and was succeeded by Messervy, transferred from command of 4th Indian Division. A few weeks later, Rommel attacked the division and threw it into confusion, the operations which followed having resulted in withdrawal to the Gazala line. Lumsden laid much of the blame for the disaster on Messervy. He was determined not only that his division should, at last, fight as a whole, with both its armoured brigades, but also that, if co-operation with Messervy was inevitable, at least neither of his brigades should be placed under the latter's command. That Messervy's one armoured brigade, the 4th, contained as many Grant tanks as his two, was an additional reason for reluctance to go to his assistance. Norrie knew that his case had to be a cast-iron one, if he were not to have difficulty in imposing his will on a reluctant Lumsden, not an easy task at any time.

What then of Messervy's state of mind? Unfortunately there is no 7th Armoured Division document which affords a clue. Messervy's statement to Correlli Barnett[14] is suspect. Like most of his statements quoted in that book, it is affected by the desire to justify his own actions, a failing to which soldiers, like others, are prone. If it is true that he had always expected the main attack to come on his front, his conduct during 26/27 May, as will be related, is open to even greater criticism than would have been the case if he, like others, had believed that a move round the south would probably be a feint. Although not conclusive proof, 4th Armoured Brigade's Operation Order No. 6 of 22 May[15] gives a clue to the thinking within the division. It stated that there were three main courses open to the enemy:

(a) Along the coast and escarpment. The shortest route, but we are strongest there;
(b) The general line of the TRIGH CAPUZZO. The present dispositions of the enemy and the comparative weakness of our positions in this area tend to make this course likely;
(c) SOUTH of HACHEIM. The length and vulnerability of the enemy's L of C in this course makes it unlikely. As, however, his main strength is in his armour, he may prefer this course. Diversions are likely.

A further clue is given in the account of the events of 27 May in the regimental history of the 8th Hussars:[16]

At this juncture (0700 hrs 27 May) the Regiment were still expecting to take up their northern battle positions, and imagined that any movement to the south must be in the nature of a demonstration or a feint, as the attack was expected through the minefields north of Gazala [sic – must have meant Hacheim].

The commander of 7th Motor Brigade, Renton,[17] who succeeded Messervy in command of 7th Armoured Division on 19 June, always maintained that he had expected the main attack to come in the south. It seems odd, and somewhat inconsistent with this if an attack was regarded as imminent, that he allowed his brigade major to go on leave on 23 May and that, on 26 May, the crews of four 25-pounder guns of C Battery 4RHA, manning the brigade's position at Retma, went off to the coast to bathe and had not returned when the position was attacked the following day.[18]

It is therefore abundantly clear that there were very strong pressures, originating with Auchinleck, and permeating the intelligence staffs at all levels, influencing commanders to expect the main attack in the centre; to suspect any move round the south of Hacheim to be a feint or subsidiary action; and to be cautious about committing the armoured brigades until it was clear where the enemy's main effort was being made. The evidence given by the prisoner from 90th Light Division and other indications (including from 'Y'), that at least 21st Panzer Division had moved to the Segnali area, were discounted.

We must now turn to what actually happened.

26 May

On 26 May a *khamsin* (a southerly wind causing a dust-storm) blew, limiting tactical air reconnaissance (Tac R). At 1415 hrs 7th Armoured Division's armoured cars reported 211 MT (Motor Transport) moving north from Segnali, and, an hour later, a movement east from there, the increasing numbers of which could not be estimated owing to the dust. A quarter of an hour later 'some tanks and 12 armoured cars' were identified in the movement. This report was received at HQ 30 Corps at 1600 hrs and passed at 1615 hrs to 13 Corps, 8 Army and 1 Armd Div, Tac R being requested at the same time, confirmed as about to take off at 1700 hrs. Further reports of eastward movements were received. By the time it got dark (about 1900 hrs), the various sources of information had identified one column of 31 tanks and 60 MT, which had moved east to six miles south-west of 1st South African Division's southernmost position; another column of 17 tanks and 80 MT six miles south of that, all moving east; one of 18 tanks moving south-east, six miles south of that; and one of 10 armoured cars and 70 MT which had moved 15 miles south-east from Segnali, pushing back 4th South African Armoured Car Regiment's screen south-eastward as it did so. The number of tanks and other vehicles reported did not appear to indicate a major thrust, and most of the movement was eastward, consistent with an attack in the centre. All this information was passed both by telephone and by wireless to 8 Army, 13 Corps and 1 Armd Div. At 1900 hrs 30 Corps told 1st and 7th Armoured Divisions to implement measures concerned with Phase I, i.e. the enemy's approach to contact, but the four-hour notice to move was not shortened. The result of the Tac R was disappointing. It went too far west and saw a large camp at Asida and nothing elsewhere. Tac R was requested at first light along the inter-corps boundary (roughly the Trigh Capuzzo) to Cherima, then Segnali-Asida and back to Gambut, which would bring it over Bir Hacheim. HQ Eighth Army altered this to Tmimi-Cherima and then along the route requested. Thirteenth Corps's last-light situation report assessed the number of tanks seen on their front as 30–50 reported by 1st South African (of which two which ran onto mines were definitely identified as German) and 45 by 50th Division, of which 25 were thought to be the same as the 31 in the most northerly column reported by 7th Armoured Division. The only other information received by HQ 30 Corps before midnight was that flares had been dropped on Bir Hacheim at 2100 hrs, interpreted as 'probably a guide to movement'. Seventh Armoured Division's war diary,[19] written some time after the event, records that Messervy discussed the situation at 2130 hrs by telephone with his brigade commanders.

27 May

At 0100 hrs on 27 May 7th Armoured Division reported that at 2250 hrs 4SAAC had heard 'loud sound of vehicle movement' 12 miles south-east of Segnali, and at 0145 hrs that 'enemy columns moved south from area last reported'; that 4SAAC's patrol line had moved back five miles; that 7th Motor Brigade's two columns supporting them were being withdrawn to ten miles west of Bir Hacheim, and that the French column had reverted to command of the Free French Brigade. 30 Corps signal log[20] records that this information was passed by telephone to 1 Armd Div and 13 Corps, and by signal also to them and to Eighth Army, but 1st Armoured Division's war diary[21] does not record its receipt.

At 0215 hrs 7th Armoured Division reported to 30 Corps that 4th Armoured Brigade was standing to. In fact it was ordered at 0240 hrs to stand to and be at 15 minutes' notice to move *from first light*, and at 0320 hrs the division reported that it had ordered continuous watch to be maintained on all wireless nets. At 0430 hrs the division formally reported a summary of the information which had been coming in over the previous two-and-a-half hours from 4SAAC through 7th Motor Brigade, the headquarters of which was on the move back to its position at Retma. I had had a wireless set listening in to these, and, to his annoyance, had rung up the GSO 1 of 7th Armoured Division, Pyman,[22] to suggest that Messervy should ring up Norrie and discuss the situation. The armoured cars had reported at 2305 hrs the sound of tracked vehicles moving south-east about 15 miles west of Hacheim; at 0030 hrs, some ten miles south of that, another column moving south, and at 0130 hrs 'columns moving east' ten miles west of Hacheim. At 0435 hrs the division reported that these columns were 'making progress'; that the southerly column, believed to be German, was now 20 miles south of Bir Hacheim and that there was another one five miles west of it. All this information was passed immediately to Eighth Army, 13 Corps and 1 Armd Div, the last recording the 0430 hrs report as having been received at 0457 hrs; but the 0435 hrs one as not received until 0610 hrs, the latter, perhaps, the confirmatory signal, the telephone report not having been recorded, as it should have been, in the log.[23]

I had become increasingly convinced during the night that these movements represented the main threat, and was disturbed by Pyman's apparent complacency, suggesting that armoured cars at night could only rely on what they heard and were liable to exaggerate numbers. I warned Pyman that I was going to wake up Norrie again (I had done so at 0215 hrs) and get him to ring Messervy. I tried to persuade Norrie to ring Lumsden also to ensure that one of his brigades would be ready to move to support 7th Armoured

Division at first light, but, after he had talked to Messervy, who took the same line as Pyman had with me, he said he would not do so, as the movement reported could be the feint that everybody had predicted.

At stand-to at 0545 hrs the brigade major of 4th Armoured Brigade telephoned 7th Armoured Division and spoke to Messervy, who said that enemy columns, strength unknown, were, as they had been reported at 0435 hrs, 25 miles south-south-west of the brigade's leaguer area.[24] Three-quarters of an hour later the alarm bells began to ring, the first being a report by 3rd Indian Motor Brigade that they were being attacked by 'a whole bloody German armoured division'. It was in fact the Italian Ariete armoured division. At 0645 hrs armoured cars reported 100 tanks and 900 MT south and south-east of the Indians, 74 tanks and 200 MT 12 miles south of that, moving east, and at 0700 hrs another column of 40 tanks and 200 MT four miles to the north of the latter: a total of 247 tanks reported in the area, the nearest being only ten miles from 4th Armoured Brigade's leaguer area, where the tank crews were taking the opportunity after stand-to, in the absence of any orders to move, to brew-up their breakfast. On receipt of this alarming information, soon confirmed by Tac R as a 'mass of vehicles, including 400 tanks, some miles south of Hacheim', Messervy ordered Richards[25] to move 4th Armoured Brigade immediately to its battle position *Larwood*, north of Retma, which was only a few miles south-east of its leaguer area. Five minutes later this was changed to battle position *Majority*, close to 3rd Indian Motor Brigade. The order to regiments to form up for the move appears, from the 8th Hussars account already quoted, to have been received by them at about 0720 hrs, and, if Roberts[26] account of 3rd Royal Tank Regiment's experience is correct, there was no great urgency behind it, as they were told to 'be in position at the RV [rendezvous] at 0815 hrs'. All the accounts agree that they had only just started from their leaguer area to form up for the move when German tanks were seen approaching two miles away, and it was not long before both 8th Hussars and 3rd Royal Tanks were hotly engaged. Their accounts, quoted in my book *Tobruk*,[27] give a graphic description of what ensued.

The first-light information about the enemy was received at HQ 30 Corps between 0700 and 0710 hrs and immediately passed by signal to Eighth Army, 13th Corps and 1st Armoured Division, to the last also by telephone. My clear recollection is that Norrie rang Lumsden with the intention of ordering the latter to move 22nd Armoured Brigade to join 7th Armoured Division, and that he had an acrimonious exchange, Lumsden insisting that, as his division was still at four hours notice, none of it could move until 0830 hrs at the earliest. This seems to be borne out by the entry in 30 Corps log (0700–0710): '1 Armd Div to stand to',[28] and in 1 Armd Div log[29] at 0715 hrs: 'From 30 Corps. Plan to start Phase B. 1 Armd Div asked if still at 4 hours notice.' There is no mention of any orders to move either 22nd or 2nd Armoured Brigade until an entry in 1 Armd Div log: '0900 hrs. Div ordered to prepare to move as quickly as possible south. Comd 2 Armd Bde present [at] Main Div HQ and given verbal sitrep and warning to prepare southern move of his brigade to east of 22 Armd Bde.' The latter's war diary[30] records having received the 0700 hrs information at 0755 hrs and that liaison officers were immediately sent out, warning the brigade to be at instant readiness and for OPs (observation posts) to take up position.

Events in 7th Armoured Division's area were now moving fast. At 0800 hrs the division reported two columns moving east, south of 7th Motor Brigade's position at Retma, one being engaged by them, the other of 50 tanks. Twenty-second Armoured Brigade recorded receipt of this information at 0830 hrs. A minute later, a column, under 22nd Brigade's command, formed from 50th Division's Reconnaissance Regiment, reported 40 tanks six miles to the south, half-way between them and 3rd Indian Motor Brigade, which by this time, although nobody realized it, had been overrun. At 0845 hrs the brigade was ordered to move to a nearby battle position 'to counter the enemy's approach from the south', and at 0907 hrs, just as it was starting to do so, it was engaged by a reported 40 tanks (in fact it was the whole of 21st Panzer Division). In spite of this (probably because he had been on his way back from HQ 1st Armoured Division), it was not until 0945 hrs that Briggs,[45] Commander of 2nd Armoured Brigade, summoned his regimental commanders to an order group and gave them orders to move south to help 22nd Brigade. They did not actually do so until 1100 hrs, by which time two of 22nd Brigade's regiments, all three of which were widely separated from each other, were in grave difficulties.

They were not the only ones. Eighth Hussars and 3rd Royal Tanks in 4th Armoured Brigade had both lost almost all their Grant tanks, and, although 5th Royal Tanks had hardly been engaged at all, Richards withdrew his brigade several miles to the north-east to avoid being outflanked. At 0845 hrs, a quarter of an hour after Renton and his headquarters had rejoined the bulk of his brigade at Retma, having made a wide detour to the south during the night to avoid the enemy columns, the position was attacked by 90th Light Division. By 0930 hrs Renton decided that it was not possible to restore the situation by counter-attack, and ordered his brigade to withdraw to Bir Gubi, leaving behind two companies, four 25-pounder guns and eight of the precious new 6-pounder anti-tank guns. It is not clear whether either Richards or Renton had received Messervy's permission to withdraw, as shortly after 1000 hrs HQ 7th Armoured Division went off the air. At 0915 hrs they had reported that they were moving north-east, from the location shown on Map 5, as 25 tanks had been reported five miles south-west of them. While they were on the move, they were attacked and dispersed by a German reconnaissance unit, the operations command vehicle being knocked out and Messervy and Pyman taken prisoner. However, they had removed their badges of rank and escaped after dark. At the most crucial moment of the battle, the whole southern flank, except for the Free French, who beat off an attack by 50 Italian tanks, had now collapsed. Norrie, and therefore Ritchie also, was suddenly deprived not only of all information of what was going on, but also any means of influencing it, except through 1st Armoured Division.

We must now consider how much Ritchie knew of what had happened. There is no evidence about whether or when he was woken up to be told of the information which had been passed on during the night from HQ 30 Corps. Eighth Army's war diary[31] records at 0420 hrs 27 May the receipt of 30 Corps sitrep originated at 0150 hrs, reporting that 'enemy columns, including tracked vehicles, had moved south'. In spite of the fact that the 30 Corps log records that all information received from 7th Armoured Division during the night was passed to HQ Eighth Army, the next entry in the latter's war diary refers to a telephone call from Norrie at 0830 hrs, reporting that between 211 and 230 tanks had been seen that morning on 30 Corps's front; that an enemy column was engaging 7th Motor Brigade's 'box' at Retma; that the Free French Brigade and (surprisingly) 3rd Indian Motor Brigade had not yet been engaged, and that 4th Armoured Brigade was moving south. Half-an-hour later it records a further telephone call from 30 Corps, reporting that all the tanks south of Bir Hacheim were German, and that Norrie considered it as the main thrust; that they had 'got through 3rd Indian Motor Brigade and [were] still worrying them'; that 4th Armoured Brigade was in contact; that 1st Armoured Division was being moved, one armoured brigade to the west and one to the east of 4th Armoured Brigade, and that there were 251 tanks due south of Hacheim. At 0930 hrs Norrie rang again, reporting that 22nd Armoured Brigade had attacked 40 tanks just south of their leaguer area.[32] At 1045 hrs Ritchie signalled the C-in-C,[33] saying that at 0930 hrs 30 Corps reported that about 250 German tanks, after a night march south of Hacheim of some 40 miles, were being engaged by 1 and 7 Armoured Divisions in the area 10–20 miles east of Hacheim, and that a few Italian tanks had been sent west of that place; that 7th Motor Brigade had been engaged at Retma, but that the Free French, 3rd Indian Motor and 29th Indian Brigades had not been; that there had been a demonstration on the front of 1st South African Division and little activity on that of the 50th. He concluded:

I appreciate that enemy thrust is between GUBI and HACHEIM directed on EL ADEM. That he is using ARIETE to protect his line of supply from SEGNALI against attacks by 50 Div and Free French Brigade. I have ordered 50 Div to act boldly with columns against enemy MT. Air support is being concentrated on area south track GUBI-HACHEIM.

Auchinleck replied to this in two signals, the first,[34] originated at 1545 hrs, said:

Many thanks your U998. You were right and I was wrong. I give you best. Agree your last appreciation but watch out for favourite PINCER movement possibly tonight against extreme NORTH flank and coast. Hit him hard. Good luck.

The second originated at 1650 hrs went:

I agree with your appreciation but in view our estimate total enemy strength would not repeat not rule out second attack by tanks etc against front one SA Div this evening or to-night coupled with attempted landing on coast EAST of GAZALA. This would be in accordance with PINCER principle and he may hope to have drawn off all our tanks far to SOUTH. Give you this for what it is worth and am sure you have it in mind.

A dense fog of war now cloaked the battlefield. Receiving no further signals from 7th Armoured Division, Norrie left his main headquarters, which, in order to avoid the same fate as Messervy's, moved 20 miles north-east to near Sidi Rezegh, and made his way to join Lumsden. Ritchie left his main headquarters at 1100 hrs for Gott's headquarters at El Adem, which he did not reach until 1330 hrs. On the way he came across HQ 4th Armoured Brigade, and, in the light of what Richards told him and of reports he had received of enemy columns approaching No. 4 Forward Base (90th Light Division reported to Rommel at 1000 hrs that they had reached El Adem), he ordered Richards to move towards Belhamed and deal with this threat. On arrival at HQ 13th Corps, he received a misleading and out-of-date report from his main headquarters that 29th Indian, 1st Free French and (indecipherable) Motor Brigade were all 'OK'; that the armoured battle was moving north and towards El Adem; that there was a separate armoured battle in the Knightsbridge (201 Guards Brigade)[36] area, and that HQ 30 Corps had moved to Sidi Rezegh. Shortly before he left Gott's headquarters at 1600 hrs, he received a message from his main headquarters that 7th Motor Brigade had been overrun and had withdrawn to Bir Gubi. He was given an accurate location for main HQ 30 Corps, where the BGS was, but told that Norrie himself was 'in the El Adem area' and that 'enemy force plus armoured division' (?of the strength of an armoured division plus?) was 'moving up EL ADEM track'. He had established his tactical headquarters close to Gott's, where he could not have welcomed a message from Auchinleck which reached him from his main headquarters at 2000 hrs, reminding him of the possibility of an attack on 1st South African Division and of an amphibious landing. At 2030 hrs he walked over to Gott's headquarters, to which Norrie had now brought his tactical headquarters, and, when he returned at 2145 hrs he told his staff that the orders he had given them were:

(1) to establish a defensive line along the escarpments south of Sidi Rezegh to ensure the safety of 4 Forward Base;

(2) after the enemy had been chased off this line, 4th Armoured Brigade was to move to the area NW of El Adem and come under command of 1st Armoured Division, if 7th Armoured Division was still incapable of functioning;

(3) 1st Armoured Division was to continue the battle in their area until the enemy east of El Adem had been cleared up.

These orders were unnecessarily defensive; but, in the light of the paucity of information, the depressing report from Norrie of the state of his Corps, and the uncertainty about the situation in the vulnerable area which included the forward base, his main headquarters and the forward airfields (4th Armoured Brigade had engaged enemy north of Sidi Rezegh at last light), he can hardly be blamed for trying to ensure that his Army was 'properly balanced', as Montgomery would have put it. If he had realized what a mess Rommel had got himself into, which the Rommel Papers make clear,[37] and that, in spite of the casualties which both Norrie's armoured divisions had suffered, they had inflicted significant casualties on the Afrika Korps, he should have urged Norrie, and perhaps Gott also, to adopt a more offensive attitude next day. In the following fortnight he was to be criticized for being too optimistic. Had he been less prudent and urged bolder action that night, it *might* possibly have produced better results; but his subordinates were in a defensive mood. Lumsden had gathered his bewildered and battered armoured brigades around the safe haven of the Guards Brigade 'box' at Knightsbridge. Messervy was presumed to be in captivity, and, of Messervy's subordinates, Renton was sitting impassive at Bir Gubi, and Richards, who had spent the day ordering successive withdrawals, was trying to find his supply echelons near Sidi Rezegh. Auchinleck was suggesting that Rommel's main thrust had still not been delivered and that it might come as an assault on Pienaar's 1st South African Division, in whom, and in whose commander (in view of his performance in command of 1st

South African Brigade in the *Crusader* operation in the previous autumn) neither Gott nor Ritchie, with justification, had great confidence. Even if Ritchie had ordered bold counter-offensive action, he would have been unrealistic in expecting much to come of it.

The events of 27 May 1942, and those leading up to it, have been discussed in detail, because it is on Ritchie's plan for the defence of Eighth Army's position and on its execution that his critics have concentrated their attacks. Whether one is pro- or anti-Ritchie, one must face the question of what he, personally, could have done to alter the disastrous course of events on that critical day of 27 May, before one tackles the question of what he could have then done to remedy it. One is forced to the conclusion that, unless one accepts that the basic plan was faulty, there was little or nothing that Ritchie could have done, from the time that the enemy's advance was first detected in the afternoon of 26 May to the end of the following day, to influence events, although he, in contrast to almost all the other commanders at every level from C-in-C to brigade commander, and in spite of expert intelligence assessments, foresaw the course that Rommel would follow.

Was the course of events due therefore to Ritchie's failure to accept Auchinleck's advice, as the majority of authors who have described the campaign – Agar-Hamilton and Turner, Connell, Barnett, Jackson, Warner, Parkinson: all, but the first, what one might call the 'pro-Auk lobby' – have suggested: advice that Gott should assume responsibility for all the static defensive positions and that 7th Armoured Division should be relieved of its task of 'protecting the southern flank' and should move 4th Armoured Brigade 12 miles further north in order that the armour should be concentrated?

Ritchie had accepted the principle that 7th Armoured Division should be relieved of the flank protection task, and he awaited the arrival of Tuker to implement it; but, for good practical reasons, including the range of wireless sets, particularly at night, but also on other grounds, including the command of those essential providers of information, the armoured car regiments, he rightly resisted handing over responsibility for co-ordinating operations over the whole vast front to Gott's 13th Corps, which was primarily an infantry formation. It is unlikely that the outcome would have been very different if 4th Armoured Brigade had been located further north, whether or not 7th Armoured Division had been relieved of the flank protection task. It might have been, now that we know what Rommel's plan was; but it might well not. Assuming that, by about 0700 hrs on 27 May, Norrie would have realized that the Afrika Korps was south-east of Bir Hacheim, it is doubtful if he would have been able to reorient Lumsden's brigades in time for them, and 4th Armoured Brigade, to be in battle positions facing south-east between the minefields and El Adem. If he had been able to achieve this – and the delay in getting 1st Armoured Division into action does not lead one to suppose that he would – what would Rommel have done? Ninetieth Light Division would have had an unopposed run to Sidi Rezegh, and, impetuous exploiter of success as he always was, the likelihood is that Rommel would have held off all Norrie's armour with 21st Panzer and Ariete Divisions and switched 15th Panzer to join 90th Light. That would have produced chaos in Eighth Army's rear area, and the ineffective performance of Norrie's armour, when it turned to the attack in subsequent days, does not lead one to suppose that it would have fared any better in a counter-attack to cut them off. It would have been imprudent in the extreme for Ritchie to have run the risk of Rommel having a clear, unopposed run into his vulnerable rear area. One must appreciate that the area behind the combat troops was littered with soft-skinned vehicles, some belonging to the fighting units and others forming headquarters, communication and logistic units of every kind. They had no means of defending themselves against tanks or guns other than movement, and that was not always possible at short notice. The notion, therefore, that Ritchie was primarily to blame for the near-disastrous events of 27 May, and that, if he had accepted the advice in Auchinleck's letter of 20 May, all would have been well, is in my view mistaken. Indeed, the boot is on the other foot. If Auchinleck had not used his authority to try and predict Rommel's plan, all concerned would have been less reluctant to accept that the enemy moves reported during the night might be his main thrust, and have taken more urgent action to ensure that the armoured brigades of 30th Corps were ready, as dawn broke on 27 May, to meet it.

We must now turn to the accusation that Ritchie's attempts to turn the tables on Rommel between 28 May and 13 June were ineffective, and that he was consistently over-optimistic. Ineffective they certainly were, and it is true that he remained optimistic; but others below Ritchie's level contributed heavily to ineffectiveness in the execution of Ritchie's orders, at times contributing to his optimism, at others indulging in undue pessimism.

28 May

Dawn on 28 May revealed a concentration, reported as of 155 tanks, a few miles north of the Guards Brigade. Twenty-second Armoured Brigade was just east of this concentration, while the 2nd was immediately south-east of the Guards, a few miles to the south of the 22nd. North of the escarpment, a column, commanded by 8th Royal Tanks and including 15 Valentine tanks, was placed under Lumsden's command. His orders, issued at 0425 hrs, had been that, once the position to the north and north-west had been cleared up, the armoured brigades would 'clear to southeast and south and then move east'.[38] However, when daylight revealed the presence of the 155 tanks, Lumsden adopted a defensive attitude. The concentration was in fact 15th Panzer Division with 43 tanks out of fuel, 14 of which were non-runners, and 21st, with about 100 tanks and some fuel. The latter was under orders to continue Rommel's plan to advance north and cut off 13th Corps. Lumsden had 105 Crusaders and 38 Grants in his two brigades, and was not inclined to attack the Afrika Korps. Norrie, characteristically, did not exert pressure on him to do so. Messervy and his operational staff were still missing, believed captured – they turned up at midday – and Richards, directly under Norrie's command, was dealing with 90th Light Division (thought erroneously to be only part of it) near El Adem. At about 1000 hrs Lumsden asked for every available gun that could be brought to bear, as well as air attack, to be concentrated on the enemy tanks. (The latter did not take place until the afternoon and claimed success.) Twenty-first Panzer had actually moved north at 0800 hrs without hindrance, and attacked and scattered the 8th Royal Tanks column, destroying nine of its Valentines. It then overran the 141-strong garrison of 'Commonwealth Keep', a post on the northern escarpment. It is not clear whether anybody in 1st Armoured Division realized that 21st Panzer had moved. At 1020 hrs Lumsden told Norrie that his intention was to keep his two armoured brigades in position east of the enemy and get 8th Royal Tanks (actually only one squadron) into action from the north. 'If the guns could get them on the move', he said, 'our tanks would then have an opportunity of attacking him advantageously before the enemy dig themselves in.'[39] In the event 22nd Armoured Brigade spent all day gazing at the helpless 43 tanks of 15th Panzer Division, while the Guards Motor Brigade remained stolidly static within their fortress of Knightsbridge, as they did for the next fortnight.

By midday Norrie was able, for the first time, to give Ritchie a fairly accurate picture of where the enemy formations were. It was clear to them both that Rommel had got the Afrika Korps into an awkward position, and that it was essential to close the jaws of the trap round them and cut them off from supply. All Ritchie's efforts over the next few days were directed to that end. The Rommel Papers[40] confirm that that was just what Rommel feared, and that Ritchie was not being over-optimistic in pursuing that aim. If anybody was to be accused of over-optimism it was Auchinleck and his staff in Cairo. After a conference at GHQ in the evening of 28 May, Auchinleck wrote a letter to Ritchie, which began:

As a result of Acroma [sic] battle, enemy original armoured attacking force practically wiped out. Enemy left with, say: 100 Italian tanks – in arena, and some escaped. 50–60 German tanks – TEMRAD area [the area *west* of 1st South African Division, where it had been thought that the Afrika Korps had been up to 26 May]. Four Italian divisions of about 4–5000 men (strength May 27) and 20 field guns and 15 anti-tank guns each.

Having made a more or less accurate estimate of the tanks left to Ritchie, although glossing over the fact that losses in Grants had been particularly severe, he counted into Ritchie's resources 1st Armoured Brigade, which was in Cairo on 27 May and the first regiment of which was not available to Ritchie until 3 June. Auchinleck said his object was 'to destroy the enemy army as soon as possible, so as to prevent it slipping away to the west', and gave Segnali as the first objective, while

all available light mobile forces should strike hard at Mechili and even Benghazi, while 50th Division, supported by all the 'I' tanks, thrust to Bir Temrad and 1st South African Division demonstrated in the area of the coast road in order to tie the enemy down there, so that they could be totally surrounded.[41]

29 May

When Dorman-Smith arrived with this letter at Gambut on 29 May, Ritchie was up at El Adem, conferring with Gott and Norrie, whose tanks were locked in battle all day with all of Rommel's in the area south of Knightsbridge, where 90th Light Division had rejoined the panzer divisions. Unfortunately 4th Armoured Brigade, which had pursued the division the day before, had been withdrawn to replenish during the night and then held in reserve west of El Adem, while Messervy, who had reappeared, got his division together again during the morning. Ritchie's aim was for Lumsden to link up with 150th Brigade of 50th Division and thus close the jaws of the trap; but, by the end of the day, this had not been achieved. Lumsden was slow to bring 22nd Armoured Brigade into the battle, the brunt of which was borne by two regiments of 2nd Armoured Brigade, the third being only slightly engaged. When, at midday, Norrie ordered Messervy to send 4th Armoured Brigade forward to join Lumsden, a sandstorm blew up, which prevented Richards from meeting Lumsden personally and delayed the move of his brigade, which did not get into action against 90th Light until the late afternoon, and then with little success. If blame is to be attached to anyone for the failure to close the jaws of the trap behind the Afrika Korps that day, it should be attributed to Norrie and Lumsden for not ensuring that the resources available to them were concentrated sooner and more effectively in a concerted effort.

30 May

Rommel had now decided that he must concentrate on opening up a supply route through the minefields, where the Italian Trieste division had already cleared a gap south of 150 Brigade's position, to the concern of the latter's commander, who had been reinforced by the presence of 1st Army Tank Brigade with three squadron of Matildas. Rommel therefore ordered his divisions to withdraw slightly into a defensive crescent, holding off Norrie's tanks while he secured his supply line, and they moved into their positions at dawn on 30 May. Unfortunately this was interpreted at HQ Eighth Army and elsewhere as an indication that Rommel was intending to withdraw behind the minefields, and thoughts turned towards Auchinleck's concept of a wide sweep round Hacheim, combined with a westward attack by 13th Corps. This attitude, combined with 1st Armoured Division's preoccupation with reorganizing its armour after the previous day's action – 10th Hussars had been reduced to only three tanks, which they handed over to 9th Lancers, who had lost all their Crusaders – meant that, as Rommel put it in his diary: 'The enemy [i.e. the British] was very hesitant in following up our movements.'[42] It was also unfortunate that a report that 25 German tanks were being towed away south of Hacheim led to 4th Armoured Brigade being sent off on a wild-goose chase in that direction.

The apparent lack of urgency led Ritchie to telephone Norrie at 1215 hrs to ask what Lumsden was doing. Norrie's reply was:

Very well. There is a tank battle going on SW of Knightsbridge. I think the enemy are definitely withdrawing West and NW. I have asked 1st Armoured Division, who are attacking from the east, to put their left shoulder forward and try and cut the enemy off from the gap in the Minefield.[43]

'Very well' was far from being the case. Two attempts by 2nd Armoured Brigade, helped by part of 22nd, failed, its total tank strength falling to 30 by the end of the day, as a result of which all the remaining tanks were concentrated in one composite regiment, a reorganization which had also been forced on 22nd Brigade. As a result of the casualties his armoured regiments had suffered in trying to attack the enemy, Lumsden had come to the conclusion that tanks should not be used to attack anti-tank guns, a task that should be left to the infantry, preferably to those of another formation, and he managed to persuade Norrie to issue an order to that effect on 31 May.

The true state of affairs at the end of 30 May is not reflected in the telephone conversation between Ritchie and Norrie at 1730 hrs, when Ritchie was at Norrie's tactical headquarters. It is not clear where Norrie was. The war diary[44] records that

Comd 30 Corps suggested 7 Motor Bde be moved up to pass through the minefield between 50 and 1 SA Divs, Free French attacking from the south. Comd 30 Corps stated that Gap was like a second Derby Day with all traffic trying to get through one gate. About 100 tanks had already got through. 1 Armd Div being ordered to follow and pursue the retreating enemy as hard as possible.

This sort of information, confirmed by Tac R, led to the complacent assessment in HQ Eighth Army's Intelligence Summary (Intsum) covering the period 0800 hrs 30 to 0800 hrs 31 May:

General Rommel's predeliction for flank attacks, which was described as the principal characteristic of his tactics before his arrival in AFRICA appears on this occasion to have led to his undoing. Although captured documents establish that 11 days' supply were to be carried by the encircling columns, prisoners from supply colns state that only 3 or 4 days' supplies were actually carried. Water for 4 days was carried. This meant that, unless by 30 May the enemy had succeeded in his objectives, or at least opened up an effective and protected line of supply, he would be forced to withdraw. His failure either to overcome our armoured forces, or to open up a supply line, has so far determined the battle. The only question remaining appears to be how much, in the final event, he will be able to recover and reinforce.[45]

The same summary estimated that 225 German and 70 Italian tanks had been destroyed since 26 May.

Rommel's thoughts were not on withdrawal. The vehicles 'streaming through the gap' were no doubt his empty supply vehicles returning to replenish. He had himself driven through to meet Kesselring and the commander of the Italian 10th Corps. While the Afrika Korps held off attacks from the north-east, he was going to 'clear up the southern part of the Gazala line and then resume the offensive'.[46] This would involve attacking first 150 Brigade's position, just north of the gap, and then the Free French at Bir Hacheim.

Given the information he was receiving, and the assessment of it by his intelligence staff, Ritchie cannot be blamed if his attention was concentrated on trying to implement the general plan proposed by Auchinleck, code-worded LIMERICK, which he was trying to get started on the night 31 May/1 June. On the previous evening, 29 May, he had received a signal from Auchinleck saying:

Well done. If he tries breaking out take any risk to prevent him. He must not get out. If possible and if, repeat if, you agree give following to Comdrs and troops from me: 'Well done indeed Eighth Army. Stick to it. Hang on to him. Never leave him. Do not let him get away. Give him no rest. Good luck to you all.' Good luck to you Neil.

Ritchie's reply to this, originated from his tactical headquarters at 1305 hrs

30 May, reveals the thoughts which were uppermost in his mind, following a meeting he had held at 0600 hrs with Gott and Norrie at the former's headquarters.

Sudden minor indications possibility enemy intended withdrawing necessitated me leaving Main HQ last night to be with Corps Commanders. Consequently had to leave without discussing your suggestions with D.C.G.S. [Dorman-Smith]. Jock [Whitely, BGS at HQ Eighth Army][48] will have done so. Armoured battle raged throughout yesterday in bad dust storm vicinity KNIGHTSBRIDGE – BIR EL HARMAT – BIR EL RIGEL. Results difficult to ascertain accurately due poor visibility but estimate we knocked out (though not all utterly destroyed) 85 German tanks. I estimate our casualties to have been 100 tanks (but this may be an over-estimate) and our strength today is about 150 Cruisers and 110 'I' tanks. 1 Armd Div last night estimate 150 German tanks leaguered in area (three miles south of KNIGHTSBRIDGE). Other small packets of tanks were in the 'Arena' together with much MT. Yesterday's battle was I consider well handled by Lumsden and Norrie launched 4 Armd Bde from reserve at very suitable moment. Yesterday I feel we destroyed and damaged a great deal of enemy MT and our colns were active in 'Arena' and against his line of supply.

Today I have not sufficient information to say whether or not enemy is trying to draw off but everything is aiming at stopping the gap through which he might escape and all is ready to cling to him continually. I hope shortly to get more ground information. In outline plan for offensive envisaged is [sic] 13 Corps opening route TEMRAD – SIDI BREGISC – with 1 SA, 50 Divs and all 'I' tanks and on to line TMIMI – CHECHIBAN – ROTONDA AFRAG (15 miles SW of TMIMI) if possible, while 30 Corps protects left flank. Then passing 5 Ind Div through to consolidate and operate from there into JEBEL. Armour directed on MECHILI thereafter operating against enemy flanks and rear in JEBEL or attacks enemy armour as comparative strengths and situation generally dictates. But ball will be started rolling by all our cruiser force debouching from our positions either via Route TRIGH CAPUZZO or between 1 SA and 50 Divs dependent on enemy's line of withdrawal. All plans laid and we can start quickly. Our experience 1941 and 1942 has shown error of putting semi-trained and armoured formations of undesert-worthy personnel into desert operations. Much as I dislike it I hope you will agree to allowing me liberty of action to draw on 1 Armd Bde Gps tanks and equipment to complete fully armoured formations who have thoroughly trained 'unhorsed' personnel.[49] May I have most urgent reply. Message just in. Enemy appears to be trying to break out West through minefield. Pray he does not escape. We will watch out for the dangers of a rebound.[50]

Unfortunately both Auchinleck and Ritchie were living in cloud cuckoo land. While their thoughts were directed onto these ambitious plans, Ritchie can hardly be blamed for failure to anticipate the attack on 150 Brigade, which began on that afternoon, 30 May, when none of his subordinates appeared greatly concerned about the situation.

31 May

At 0830 hrs on 31 May Ritchie conferred with his corps commanders again about the way to implement Operation LIMERICK. Contrary to Auchinleck's assumption, Rommel still had at least 100 tanks east of the minefields; and Ritchie was persuaded by Gott and Norrie that, with the weakened state of his own armour, he could not afford to move it round south of Bir Hacheim, but must keep it positioned so that it could prevent the Afrika Korps from making a renewed thrust to El Adem. The outflanking move would have to be made by a wheeled force, and suggestions were made that 5th Indian Division should be used; but there were justified doubts about its ability to undertake such an ambitious rôle. Instead it was decided that two brigades should be used to execute a night attack from south of Knightsbridge to join hands with 150 Brigade while 1st South African Division attacked westward on its front, to be followed up by 5th Indian along the coast. In his signal CS 1152, originated at 1210 hrs 31 May, Auchinleck said: 'Have heard of your plans from Dorman-Smith and like them. Supremely important that enemy shall have no, repeat no, breathing space.' Gott and Norrie, however, insisted that moves and preparations could not be completed in time for the attack to take place that night, and at 1730 hrs Ritchie reluctantly agreed to a 24-hour postponement, while '7 Motor Brigade's operation through the minefield and southern sweep on TRIESTE would start to-night.' The latter appears to refer, not to Norrie's previous suggestion, but to the action of columns drawn from 7th Motor Brigade round behind Bir Hacheim.

The idea that Rommel was intent on withdrawal had been reinforced by a message from 1st Armoured Division at 1300 hrs that 'enemy is streaming out of gap in minefield to west' and the only indication that the position of 150 Brigade was threatened came in a message from 13th Corps at 1440 hrs, reporting that 50th Division was being attacked from north and north-east in two areas to the north of 150 Brigade's position, adding that 1st Army Tank Brigade 'had joined the fray' and that 1st Armoured Division was attacking from the east. In fact the brigade had been under heavy attack all day, having beaten off probing attacks on the previous afternoon. Unfortunately the brigade headquarters appears to have been out of touch with 50th Division headquarters in the morning. The only entries in the latter's war diary for 31 May are:

0900 hrs. 150 Bde out of tel comn.
1540 hrs. 150 Bde. 1200 hrs enemy attack developed
from East and NE with approx 20 tanks (rest of message
corrupt).[51]

Although various attempts had been made during the day by the remaining tanks under 13th Corps to intervene, they were in small numbers and easily held off by the Germans, as were the not very impressive activities of 1st Armoured Division. The first note of alarm appears to have reached Ritchie's headquarters at 0130 hrs 1 June. His tactical headquarters war diary records at 1330 hrs (clearly from subsequent entries an error for 0130 hrs) receipt of a message from 13th Corps, passing on one from 50th Division, which they requested should be passed personally to the Army Commander. It said: 'Situation 150 Bde serious. Enemy penetrating area. . . . Demand full support 150 Bde first light.'[52] That the seriousness of their position had not been realized at higher levels before this is clear from the signal which Ritchie sent to Auchinleck at 1550 hrs 31 May:

Vital to success to maintain 150 Bde in position hence enemy attacks on them. They have done wonderful work and are short of ammunition. Trying to get to them still by land from North and South and by air. 50 Div report best of their belief gaps were closed last night.[53]

13th Corps's message was passed to Ritchie at 0155 hrs.

S I X

THE CAULDRON

On 1 June ULTRA at last began to provide information of Rommel's intention to hold off the British with an anti-tank screen, and then counter-attack with tanks, establishing a bridgehead in the area, now known as the Cauldron, from which he would resume the offensive. Ritchie went over to see Gott at 0830 hrs, but there is no record of what was discussed or decided. It is probable that they agreed that the plans made to launch Operation LIMERICK were the best that could be done to take the pressure off 150 Brigade. All was in fact over for the brigade at about midday; but it was not until 1515 hrs that 13th Corps reported that the brigade had 'apparently been overrun'.

In spite of this setback Ritchie decided that his planned attack should go ahead, although only one brigade, the 10th, of 5th Indian Division was available to attack from the east. Unbeknown to him, Ramsden, commander of 50th Division,[1] decided that, in view of the disappearance of 150 Brigade, he could not employ 69th Brigade to attack The Cauldron from the north, and gave the task to one battalion of 151st Brigade. It is not surprising that it failed to achieve anything. Tenth Indian Brigade arrived late in its concentration area, where a sandstorm prevented it making any reconnaissance, and Messervy, under whose command it had been placed, cancelled its attack. It was time to think again.

Connell and others have castigated Ritchie for 'failure to seize the initiative' on 29, 30 and 31 May, and make much of post-war reports by Rommel's subordinates, and a British prisoner-of-war, that the Afrika Korps was at its last gasp for supplies. Ritchie *had* seized the initiative, as Auchinleck recognized in his letter, in which he referred to 'the initiative which you have wrested from him in the last week's fighting',[2] but the disappointing results of that initiative on the battlefield (partly due to his subordinates, notably Lumsden and Messervy, partly to fundamental factors, which I have described in the final chapter of my book *Tobruk*)[3] having initially forced Rommel onto the defensive, saw it drain away.

2/3 June

In reporting the situation to Auchinleck on 2 June, Ritchie stated that, in spite of the loss of 150 Brigade, he still considered the situation 'favourable to us and getting better daily'. Events certainly proved this over-optimistic, and Auchinleck's reply that night, which was brought up by his Director of Military Intelligence, de Guingand,[4] next day (3 June), showed that he did not share it. He emphasized that it was vital to prevent the initiative passing to Rommel, and suggested that 'the quickest and easiest way to shift him is by an offensive directed towards TEMRAD so as to threaten his bases, coupled with threats from SEGNALI and the south against his line of supply', and that Ritchie should 'keep at least one infantry division concentrated and complete in mobile reserve, so that you have at your disposal a really strong weapon with which to strike'. He expressed his concern at the apparent dispersion of 5th Indian Division.[5]

Ritchie did not see de Guingand and the letter he brought until after midday on 3 June, having left Gambut at 0500 hrs for a conference with Gott and Norrie at the former's headquarters at 0700 hrs, where they discussed the resuscitation of Operation *Limerick*. Ramsden, who had favoured it, no longer had enough troops to take a leading part in a thrust towards Temrad. Pienaar, the ever-pessimistic commander of 1st South African Division, refused to do so, and when Harold Briggs, commander of 5th Indian Division, was asked by Gott to consider doing so, he 'never thought harder in my life. I had to collect in the division, plan, reconnoitre and attack within thirty-six hours'.[6] His reply was to suggest, instead, that his division should 'move round south of Bir Hacheim on to Tmimi and Rommel's L of C'. Gott and Ritchie were attracted by the idea, but, when all the implications, operational and logistic, were thoroughly examined, it was rejected. Rommel, who had already moved 90th Light and Trieste divisions to attack Bir Hacheim, would have been able to slip at least some of his armour back through the minefields and deal with Briggs, who, unless he were accompanied by most of Norrie's tanks, would be very vulnerable. If the armour went with Briggs, it would open the door for a rapid thrust by the Afrika Korps to El Adem. Messervy proposed another plan: a repetition on a larger scale of the previous plan to attack The Cauldron, combined with intensification of raids by mobile columns behind Hacheim and from 13th Corps's front. The principal attack would be launched at night from the east, south of Knightsbridge, by 5th Indian Division, supported by 4th Royal Tanks (Valentines) from 4th Armoured Brigade, which would be exploited by 22nd Armoured Brigade, transferred to Messervy's command. This would coincide with an attack by 69th Brigade from 50th Division on Sidra Ridge, which formed the northern edge of The Cauldron, supported by 32nd Army Tank Brigade. Norrie wanted Gott to command the operation, but he declined. Believing that his headquarters was not well suited to exercise detailed tactical command of such an operation, Norrie, although responsible overall, delegated tactical planning and execution to Messervy and Briggs, who located their tactical headquarters together. Sixty-ninth Brigade's attack, which was in fact executed by 32nd Army Tank Brigade with only one battalion of infantry, remained under command of 13th Corps. The operation was given the codename *Aberdeen*.

It is not clear whether a fourth option was considered, which, perhaps, offered greater prospects of success than any of the others: that would have been an attack southwards by 5th Indian Division through 50th Division's sector towards Mteifel, supported by all the 'I' tanks and at least one armoured brigade. If Rommel were thus forced to withdraw the Afrika Korps from The Cauldron, the rest of Norrie's armour could follow up without risk to Ritchie's rear areas. As 50th Division drove through the Italians facing them without great difficulty, when they eventually withdrew on 14 June, 5th Indian Division should have had no great difficulty in breaking out there. One of the problems which argued against both this concept (if it was ever considered) and the resuscitated *Limerick* was that, while 5th Indian Division was concentrating and forming up, it would be very vulnerable to a counter-attack by the Afrika Korps, north from The Cauldron. A reminder of the possibility of this was given by a northward sortie on 2 June by 21st Panzer Division which scattered a squadron of 8th Royal Tanks' Valentines and knocked out 21 of 4th Armoured Brigade's tanks sent to help them. Ritchie sent a letter back to Auchinleck with de Guingand explaining his plan. In it he wrote:

.... The two alternatives appear to me to be:
(a) to resume the offensive as early as possible directed on the line TMIMI-AFRAG;
(b) to deal first with the 'cauldron'.
Of these two alternatives it had been my intention to resume the offensive and leave the armour to mask the 'cauldron' and I left this H.Q. at 5 a.m. this morning for a conference with the Corps Commanders to get this fixed up. For various reasons, with which I am dealing, replacements in armour are not coming through as quickly as they should ... the net result is that I now feel that our armour may not be able to contain the enemy while the offensive is in progress and the enemy's armour may therefore be a real danger to me being able to continue supplies forward and against the rear of the GAZALA – ALEM HAMZA position.
2. I was, as you are, most keen to carry out the offensive with the right shoulder forward, but the enemy in his present position makes it extremely difficult to form

up a division behind our present frontage between GAZALA and ALEM HAMZA without fear of its preparations being interrupted. For this reason I had to discard that plan.

3. My next idea was to make a very wide turning movement with the 5 Ind Div South of HACHEIM directed on AFRAG, but after the information I have had from the Corps Commanders today respecting the strength of our armour I cannot risk this.

4. It is absolutely essential that we should wrest from the enemy the initiative which he is now starting to exercise and this must be done at the soonest possible moment. In the circumstances I have decided that I must crush him in the 'cauldron' and the plan for doing this will be a pincer movement, one arm coming from the north with 69 Inf Bde supported by 'I' tanks, the other from the East to be carried out by 5 Ind Div supported by 4 RTR and 22 Armd Bde for exploitation. This latter will, of course, be the main thrust, the one from the North I would not bring further South than SIDRA. Much of the preparatory reconnaissance and work for the main thrust has already been covered by the operations of 10 Inf Bde and I am re-assured in my belief of the feasibility of this operation being carried out by night by the fact that Frank MESSERVY is of opinion that it is quite feasible. I hope by this means to drive a wedge through the enemy's anti-tank defences under cover of darkness and seize the ground in the vicinity of GOT EL SCERAB, and this will enable me to exploit the armour through this corridor into the rear of the enemy and close the gaps behind him. Once it is completed we will return to the offensive generally on the lines of the right shoulder forward. . . .

5. The operation I have decided to undertake is the one which can be put into action quickest and will therefore wrest the initiative from the enemy in the shortest possible time.[7]

Auchinleck replied in a signal originated at 0120 hrs 4 June, received at Headquarters Eighth Army at 0545 hrs. It read:

Many thanks for your letter. de Guingand has explained the details of the plan you now propose to carry out and your reasons for adopting it. I agree that in view of the latest figures of tanks available which are disappointing, this plan is the most practical and has the merit of being easily and speedily implemented. It is as you say absolutely essential to wrest from the enemy at the earliest possible moment the initiative he has regained.

2. I need not stress the need for careful reconnaissance and preparation for the night attack and hope you will not hesitate to ensure these even if you have to delay the operation another day. Night operations are always difficult and adequate time must be allowed.

3. I think the operation has good chance of success but infantry must have tanks in close support as soon as moon rises. New Zealanders at Sidi Rezegh learned this lesson.

4. Your proposed plan involves frontal attack always liable to be costly. This does not matter if success follows. Presume you have considered alternative of attacking from North from 50 Div positions against enemy flank. I feel this bastion has great tactical possibilities if these are properly exploited. However time may be lacking.

5. Am glad you are not unduly anxious about Bir Hacheim and hope to hear tomorrow that attack has been finally repulsed.

6. Am a bit upset by figures of tanks available in units compared with number of tanks we know to be ready for action. Suggest this needs chasing somewhere. If anyone is to blame do not let him escape.

7. Our situation map built up on liaison officers reports shows three infantry brigades in Tobruk. Is this essential? I feel it is absolutely necessary to hold ACROMA, EL Adem and Bir Hacheim and adequate garrisons should be provided for all these places. As I see it you have plenty of infantry. Have you not?

8. I feel too that it is most desirable to keep formations intact as far as possible though I realize this cannot always be done. I visualized your using 10 Indian Div as holding troops until they become acclimatized and 5 Indian complete as a striking force. However I realize one cannot help oneself sometimes, though one gets better results from an intact formation.

9. If you want reliefs for individual commanders do not hesitate to say so.

10. What about a minefield from 69 Infantry Brigade to Tamar (half-way between it and Acroma) to protect yourself from disruptive movements by enemy? Should not Tamar be made into strong point and South African troops spared from Tobruk? These are only half-baked suggestions. Good Luck.[8]

Connell does not mention Ritchie's letter, but instead expatiates on a 'six page paper' adumbrating future possible operations, prepared by Ritchie's staff, based on the assumption that current operations would be successful. He refers briefly to Auchinleck's reply and to Ritchie's assurance that the commanders concerned had had plenty of time for reconnaissance; that they had been told that they could postpone the operation for a further 24 hours beyond the planned time, the night 4/5 June; but that they had said they did not need it.

5 June

The reconnaissance unfortunately was not very thorough. It failed to locate accurately either the enemy positions, held by Ariete Division, or that of the proposed start line, from which 10th Indian Brigade launched its assault. The result was that the artillery bombardment fell on empty desert, and the attack never penetrated Ariete's positions. It merely alerted the German Panzer divisions, both of which, contrary to the intelligence estimate, with 152 tanks, were in the area. It was erroneously thought that 15th Panzer Division was with 90th Light, threatening the French at Bir Hacheim. The result was that, when the second phase began, involving a further advance by 9th Indian Brigade and 22nd Armoured Brigade, the latter met heavy anti-tank fire and veered away from the infantry, who were left helpless in the desert. Better results might have been achieved by another 24 hours of preparation, to ensure that the inexperienced infantry and the tanks, who were not accustomed to close co-operation with them, could co-ordinate detailed tactical plans, but it is doubtful if the plan ever had much prospect of success. For that Ritchie must bear the blame, although not as much as Norrie for the muddles in execution. Thirty-second Army Tank Brigade's attack ended in equal failure, and with Rommel's counter-attack in the afternoon, control of the operation collapsed, and total failure had to be accepted.

6 June

Some 3000 troops were left stranded in the area, and Norrie's attempts to rescue them next day, by placing all three armoured brigades under Messervy's command, failed to produce any effective action out of any of them. Rommel took the unfortunate 3000 prisoner, with 96 field and 37 anti-tank guns. He had knocked out 50 of 32nd Brigade's and 60 of 22nd Brigade's tanks, Norrie's total tank strength having fallen from 300 to 132 by the end of 6 June, Rommel having suffered hardly any losses, being left with 160 German and 70 Italian tanks.

However, the true picture was not revealed to Ritchie until the following morning. On the contrary, 30th Corps reported a successful day. At 1940 hrs 6 June, Hatton, the BGS, reported '2nd Armoured Brigade had a very good party yesterday evening and 22nd Armoured Brigade did very well today. 4th Armoured Brigade seem to be having a good party.' This report was followed by a signal, originated at 2053 hrs, received at Ritchie's head-quarters at 2203 hrs, stating:

Continued magnificent work achieved today. Enemy received hard knock. 1st Armoured Division with 2nd and 22nd Armoured Brigades under command will continue to deny area Eluet et Tamar to Knightsbridge. 7th Armoured Division with 4th Armoured Brigade and 10th Indian Infantry Brigade under command secure line Knightsbridge – B 100 (4 miles SW) and responsible observation south flank 30 Corps. 7th Motor Brigade acting on special orders (operating round Hacheim). 5th Indian Division provide two columns under command 7th Armoured Division.[9]

This optimistic picture was corrected by a personal signal from Norrie, originated at 0700 hrs 7 June, received at Eighth Army Headquarters at 0940 hrs. Shortly after that, General Corbett, Auchinleck's chief of staff, arrived by air at Gambut for a two-day visit.

7–10 June

Connell's criticism of Ritchie reaches a crescendo at this point.[10] He accused him of concealing from Auchinleck the true state of his losses, noting that, after 4 June, there were no more of the long personal letters that had been exchanged almost daily before that; of painting an over-optimistic picture of the situation, and of 'breaking the Army up into a thousand fragments' despite Auchinleck's insistence, in his letter of 20 May, that divisions should fight as divisions (he was then referring to the armoured divisions).

The answer to Connell's first two accusations is a simple one. Corbett's visit, which included accompanying Ritchie to Gott's headquarters to meet the corps commanders, made a 'long personal letter' unnecessary. It also refutes the accusation that Ritchie was deliberately concealing the true situation from Auchinleck. He did not know it himself until just before Corbett arrived.

The answer to the accusation of 'breaking up the Army' is more complicated. The only division which, up to this time, could be said to have been 'broken up' had been 5th Indian. At the start of the battle, one of its brigades, the 29th, was used to garrison Bir Gubi under command of 7th Armoured Division, and another, the 9th, to provide 2nd South African Division in Tobruk with a third brigade. This was to replace its own 3rd South African Brigade, which was under command of 1st South African Division, whose 5th Brigade had never been rescuscitated since it had been overrun in the *Crusader* operation. But by 5 June 5th Indian Division had all three of its own brigades under command, 29th garrisoning El Adem and 9th and 10th west of it, 11th Indian Brigade from 4th Indian Division having replaced the 9th in Tobruk. All other divisions were reasonably concentrated with their own brigades under command. In 7th Armoured Division, 7th Motor Brigade was widely separated from 4th Armoured Brigade, but that resulted from the conflicting demands of keeping all Norrie's armour as concentrated as possible and the need to give some support to the Free French at Hacheim, the maintenance of whose position both Norrie and Ritchie were beginning to feel was more of a liability than an asset.

A fundamental problem was that the infantry division was not suitably equipped and organized for operations in the desert. It was extremely vulnerable once it left the shelter of its prepared positions, surrounded by minefields, and in many parts of the desert the preparation of positions involved the use of compressed-air tools to dig in the rock. They had to face in all directions – 150 Brigade, facing west and south-west, was attacked from the north and north-east – and be stocked with food, water and ammunition if they were to resist attack. Their transport vehicles had to be sent elsewhere, if they were not to be destroyed by enemy shellfire. The infantry could not therefore easily be moved, and was very vulnerable, on foot or in vehicles, until re-established in a similar position. In their static, all-round defensive positions, often called 'boxes', they could only influence the battle within range of guns sited within the position. They could therefore be ignored, and one wonders why Rommel spent so much time and effort in attacking the Free French at Bir Hacheim. 201 Guards Brigade, the *Motor* Infantry Brigade of 1st Armoured Division, remained immobile in its 'box' at Knightsbridge from 26 May to 13 June, and, although it served a useful purpose as a rallying point for the armoured brigades, it took no other part in the battle.

There were two controversial instances of 'breaking up'. One was the establishment of brigade 'boxes'. If, for instance, 50th Division's brigades had been closer together, forming a divisional position, it would have occupied much less space and Rommel could have forced his way through the minefields more easily. The purpose that was supposed to be served by depositing brigades, like the Free French at Hacheim, 3rd Indian Motor Brigade near them, 29th Indian, first at Bir Gubi and then at El Adem, and the brigades later established in positions covering 4 Forward Base and Gambut, was to provide some form of static framework within which the armour could manoeuvre and the administrative clutter of the rear areas find some sort of refuge from the manoeuvring of the enemy armour; and also to make it more difficult for the enemy to establish himself at significant places, such as passes up and down escarpments. The trouble was that, unless the manoeuvrings of the armoured formations were successful, all these positions became hostages to fortune. If, instead, the infantry had been concentrated in divisional positions, they would have had little influence on the battle, and if the mobile battle were lost, they also would be hostages to fortune, as 2nd South African Division was in Tobruk and 1st South African and 50th would have been, if Ritchie had not been quick to order their withdrawal on 14 June, and as the Italian Divisions and some German formations had been in the *Crusader* operation in December 1941.

The other 'breaking up' issue concerned the armoured regiments and the formation of composite regiments out of squadrons of different ones. There was little alternative to this, given the rate at which tank casualties were taking place. Re-forming complete regiments would have taken too long. Ritchie pressed his energetic and able, if ruthless, GSO1(SD), Lieutenant-Colonel Belchem, himself a tank man, to restore the active tank strength in the forward area as rapidly as he could. Speed in achieving this was undoubtedly at the expense of personal and regimental considerations. This adversely affected morale, already low among tank crews as a result of their unfortunate experiences and lack of sleep. More controversial was the breaking up of 1st Armoured Brigade. Two of its regiments, 1st Royal

Tanks on 3 June and 6th Royal Tanks on 7 June, were allotted to 4th Armoured Brigade. It has been suggested that it would have been preferable to keep the brigade together as a fresh formation, perhaps replacing 4th Armoured Brigade, the performance of which had not been impressive.

It was unjust to accuse Ritchie, at this stage, of having deliberately broken up divisions. It is true that, after the fall of Tobruk, he came to the conclusion that the organization of infantry divisions was unsuitable, and that, unless they could hold a divisional defensive position with both flanks resting on the sea, their brigades should be reorganized into two elements: a forward element consisting of mobile brigades, the infantry of which acted solely as escort to the guns, and a rear element to be used for rear area defence; but it was Auchinleck, not he, who tried to implement that reorganization when he relieved Ritchie on 25 June.

If Ritchie, in spite of his difficulties, remained optimistic, he had some grounds for being so. ULTRA and Army 'Y' were now providing much more detailed information, and it was clear that Rommel was running seriously short of German infantry while Ritchie, with the arrival of 1st Armoured Brigade's regiments and tank replacements, taken from 10th Armoured Division in the process of forming in Egypt, should be able to build up his tank strength again more quickly than Rommel. Should he have turned pessimistic at that stage, as Cunningham had done at the start of *Crusader*? If so, he might have advised a withdrawal to the Egyptian frontier, or at least to the defences of Tobruk, and would undoubtedly have been dismissed if he had. The example of Cunningham was a reminder. But he was not the man to give up as long as there was a ray of hope. With the advantage of hindsight, it is now clear that, as there was no immediate hope of seizing the initiative from Rommel by a counter-attack it would have been better if, on or about 7 June, Ritchie had withdrawn 13th Corps to the line Acroma-El Adem, given up Bir Hacheim and concentrated Norrie's armour in the Sidi Rezegh area. The operation of 'columns' into Rommel's rear, by 7th Motor Brigade round south of Bir Hacheim, and by 13th Corps from their sector, on which Ritchie based exaggerated hopes while planning more ambitious armoured thrusts in both areas after the build-up of his tank strength, was ineffective. They were no more than pinpricks and had little effect on Rommel's operations, although 90th Light Division became concerned about them, delaying its attacks on the French.

Ritchie had wished to withdraw the French from Hacheim after the failure of Operation *Aberdeen*, but Auchinleck had insisted that he should continue to hold it. On 8 June Rommel sent 15th Panzer Division to join 90th Light and Trieste Divisions in the attack on the French, leaving 21st Panzer and

Ariete to threaten an attack on the Guards Brigade at Knightsbridge; the latter absorbed Norrie's attention, as he regarded it with some justification as more serious than the possible loss of the position at Hacheim. The attack on the French was intensified on 9 June, leading their commander Koenig to request, at 1700 hrs, that arrangements should be made for withdrawal that night. It could not be executed at such short notice, but, as had already been provisionally planned, it was arranged for the following night, 10/11 June, with Ritchie's approval. 2700 men, including 200 wounded, out of the original 3600, were evacuated, Rommel claiming 1000 prisoners, 24 guns and 'several hundred' vehicles. Koenig himself had left the night before.

11 June

The initiative now clearly lay with Rommel, and he lost no time in acting on it. He had a total of 226 tanks, of which 70 were Italian, 23 light tanks and 5 command tanks. His effective German combat tank strength was therefore 128. On 9 June Norrie had 200: 105 in Lumsden's two brigades, of which 44 were Grants; and 95, of which 39 were Grants, in Richards's 4th Armoured Brigade under Messervy. To the north Gott had 63 Matildas and Valentines. In numbers of men and equipment Ritchie's Eighth Army was superior to Rommel's Panzerarmee, although the tank balance was nearly even. A fuller general comparison is given in my book *Tobruk*.[12] As Norrie had antici-pated,[13] Rommel thrust north-east from Hacheim towards El Adem, with 15th Panzer Division heading for El Adem, 90th Light on its right. Twenty-first Panzer and Ariete had been told to 'demonstrate eastward' from The Cauldron to tie down Norrie's armour. Although Rommel ordered the move early in the morning of 11 June, it did not start until about 1500 hrs, harassed by columns on either flank. Fourth Armoured Brigade, which was south-east of Knightsbridge, was ordered to intervene; but having reached what he thought was a good battle position, Richards refused to go any further, and, after the exchange of some long-range fire with 15th Panzer, both sides settled down to a quiet night.

12 June

Norrie now saw an opportunity to deal with 15th Panzer on its own, and he ordered Lumsden on 12 June to send 2nd Armoured Brigade, a few miles away to the north, to join the 4th under Messervy's command. The latter was ordered to attack 15th Panzer as it resumed its advance towards El Adem, which was held by 29th Indian Infantry Brigade, while Lumsden, with 22nd Armoured and 32nd Army Tank Brigades, held off 21st Panzer and Ariete. Here at last was an opportunity, presented by Rommel's having split his armour. But Messervy had other ideas. He wanted both 2nd and 4th Armoured Brigades to pass behind 15th Panzer and join Renton's 7th Motor Brigade, so that he would take on the right flank of 15th Panzer and 90th Light's thrust, while Lumsden, facing both ways, would deal with the left flank. He set off at about 0800 hrs to try and meet Norrie, after an earlier visit to 4th Armoured Brigade. On his way he ran into a German reconnaissance unit and took refuge down a 'bir', one of the many dry water-cisterns that abounded in the desert. He could apparently still use his wireless set, and at 0905 hrs sent a message to his main headquarters telling them to order both armoured brigades to move 15 miles south from where the 4th was, and then turn east.[14] Fifteenth Panzer expected attack and, instead of resuming its advance, faced north to meet one. But neither 4th Armoured Brigade, still in the previous day's position, nor the 2nd, which had moved to join it, moved. At 0945 hrs Norrie realized what had happened to Messervy and issued orders, through main headquarters 7th Armoured Division, for 4th Armoured Brigade to move '6 or 7 miles south', with the 2nd echeloned in its rear, to attack 15th Panzer from the flank and rear.[15] At 1052 hrs Messervy signalled from his refuge: 'Put my plan into operation at earliest opportunity.'[16] At that time 1st Armoured Division reported itself as 'happy', but by 1115 hrs Lumsden was becoming concerned about concentrations of enemy south of Knightsbridge, and asked for 32nd Army Tank Brigade to be moved from the north to west of the Guards. This was eventually cleared with 13th Corps at 1345 hrs and the brigade placed under Lumsden's command. At 1200 hrs, Messervy still being missing, Norrie decided that it would be better if Lumsden took command of 4th and 22nd Armoured Brigades and asked him when he could do this. At 1238 hrs 1st Armoured Division replied that Lumsden was considering the problem. At 1305 hrs neither brigade had moved and they were told, on Norrie's orders, to 'Push on as quickly as possible and try and find a flank.' Lumsden having considered the problem, his staff agreed with that of 7th Armoured Division that command should pass at 1400 hrs; but at 1440 hrs Norrie was still telling Lumsden: '4th and 22nd Armoured Brigades will come under your command on your reaching their area. Their commanders have been ordered to attack to south to destroy the enemy,' and it was not until 1525 hrs that 1st Armoured Division reported that it had taken over. Neither brigade had moved, and at 1535 hrs 4th Armoured Brigade reported that the enemy looked like attacking their positions and asked for more pressure from the south.[17] Ten minutes later Lumsden reported that his tanks were being heavily engaged a few miles east of Knightsbridge by tanks that came from the south, and said that he proposed to 'consolidate round the Guards "box", as the armoured brigades took over in a bad state'. Norrie retorted that he must have more information of the state and position of the armoured brigades and the position of the enemy and why his original orders could not be carried out: that his intention remained to destroy the enemy armour; that Lumsden was to help 29th Indian Brigade at El Adem, if he could, but was not to let the armour get dispersed. Lumsden replied that the state of the brigades and their inability to attack south was due to tank casualties, and that he was concentrating round the Knightsbridge box. Norrie ordered that the armour was to concentrate and then be as offensive as possible. His intention remained to destroy the enemy armour. 'Cannot sit and do nothing.'[18]

Norrie received little more enlightenment about the situation until 1730 hrs, when 1st Armoured Division reported that they were engaging seven tanks eight miles south of Knightsbridge, 20 tanks three miles north-east of that, 56 in the area in which 15th Panzer had started the day, and, alarmingly, 35 on the escarpment *north* of the Trigh Capuzzo between Knightsbridge and El Adem, where, at 1840 hrs, it was reported that 4th Armoured Brigade was heavily engaging tanks. That was the last information to reach Norrie that evening. Lumsden having moved his headquarters north of the escarpment towards Acroma, speech communication by wireless between the two headquarters failed. Norrie did not know that the three armoured brigades had lost about 90 tanks, half their strength, and that the 4th had finished up north of the main escarpment. What had actually happened was that, about midday, 21st Panzer and Ariete, undetected and not interfered with by 1st Armoured Division, thrust east from The Cauldron area, south of Knightsbridge, and struck 4th Armoured Brigade in the right rear, at the same time as 15th Panzer thrust between its left flank and 2nd Armoured Brigade, pursuing Richards, as he withdrew north-east all the way to the escarpment. Ninetieth Light Division had meanwhile spent all day, under Rommel's critical eye and heavily bombed by the RAF, making ineffectual attempts to attack 29th Indian Brigade at El Adem and causing some concern for the security of the rear area to Eighth Army Headquarters, where Auchinleck was conferring with Ritchie.

The events of this decisive day in the fortunes of Eighth Army have been described in some detail because it was indeed critical; they were well recorded in 30th Corps' operations log; they illustrate clearly the sort of problem Ritchie faced in getting his intentions converted into action and in knowing what the situation was; they show the contrast between the functioning of command on the two sides, and they had a profound effect on the decisions being taken by Auchinleck and Ritchie on that day. The former flew back to Cairo after lunch on 13 June, and it is not clear how much was then known at Eighth Army Headquarters of the true state of Norrie's armour. The only clue is to be found in 8th Army Intsum covering the period 0800 hrs 12 to 0800 hrs 13 June. It stated: 'The enemy resolutely pressed on with his thrust, using 90 Light Div to threaten and attack El Adem and the Knightsbridge Box, south of the Trigh Capuzzo. No details of enemy tank losses are available, but there were evidently losses on both sides in these engagements.'[19]

Ritchie cannot be held responsible for the catastrophic turn of events. His armour was concentrated and well placed. The blame must fall on Messervy and Lumsden for the dilatory fashion in which they exercised command, and on Norrie for not being firmer in imposing his will on them, although, by the time that Lumsden did eventually take command of 2nd and 4th Armoured Brigades, it was not possible for him to 'attack south and destroy enemy armour' as Norrie ordered. Eighth Army never recovered from this setback, and if Auchinleck and Ritchie, when they were conferring together, had known what the true situation was before the C-in-C flew back on 13 June, they would probably have reversed the decision, which they had reached, not to withdraw 1st South African and 50th Divisions. It was regrettable that Auchinleck had not come up to see Ritchie immediately after the failure of Operation *Aberdeen*. If he was as worried about the situation as Connell made out, it was remiss of him not to have done so. The record of their discussion on this critical day is tantalizingly sparse. As they were together, there were no signals or letters between them, and, if staff officers were present and a record taken, there is no trace of it. All we know[20] is that Ritchie expressed his concern that, if Norrie's armour suffered defeat, Gott's forward divisions might be cut off; that he saw the choice as being between standing and fighting from his existing positions and withdrawing to the Egyptian frontier: a withdrawal could involve a running fight, and it raised the awkward question of what to do about Tobruk, which the Commanders-in-Chief Middle East, after the experience of the cost of maintaining a besieged garrison there in 1941, had decided 'must not again be invested'. Ritchie therefore recommended that he should stand and fight where he was, and Auchinleck agreed. In line with this decision was another: that all the remaining armour should be concentrated in 1st Armoured Division (as it had in fact been that afternoon) and that Lumsden should pass to Gott's command on 13 June, Norrie being left with the responsibility (without any tanks) for the defence of the rear area, from El Adem eastwards, with 5th and 10th Indian Divisions, and 7th Armoured, shorn of its only armoured brigade.

13 June

Lumsden, out of touch with any superior, had decided to stand on the defensive round Knightsbridge, with the weakened 32nd Army Tank, and 2nd and 22nd Armoured Brigades all flanking 201st Guards Brigade's 'box', while 4th Armoured licked (and it was hoped cured) its wounds behind them, north of the escarpment. Lumsden's total tank strength to effect this was about 100. Rommel's plan was for 21st Panzer to seize the Rigel ridge, north-west of Knightsbridge, where 2nd Scots Guards held an isolated 'box', while 15th thrust to the escarpment, known as Raml Ridge, north-east of Knightsbridge. Ninetieth Light was to renew its so far fruitless attack on El Adem. When this assault began in the morning of 13 June, it appeared to lack vigour, and Lumsden felt confident that he could hold both prongs; but, in the late afternoon, the attack on the Scots Guards was intensified and Lumsden ordered both 2nd and 22nd Armoured Brigades westward to support them. This coincided not only with a duststorm, but also with a renewed attack by 15th Panzer, urged on by Rommel and Nehring, commander of the Afrika Korps, in person. The jaws of Rommel's pincer now closed. The Scots Guards were forced out of their 'box', while 22nd Armoured Brigade and all the remaining tanks of the 32nd, concentrated under Foote (commanding officer of 7th Royal Tanks, whose gallantry the previous day was to earn him the Victoria Cross),[21] held 21st Panzer off the track leading from Knightsbridge to the pass down the escarpment to the north, now a narrow corridor. Lumsden asked Gott for permission to withdraw the Guards during the night, and, inevitably, it was granted. All Ritchie's remaining tanks, now reduced to 50 Grants, Stuarts and Crusaders and 20 'I' tanks, were concentrated, with the Guards Brigade, under Lumsden's command near Acroma. It was not clear at what hour Ritchie became aware of the results of the day's fighting, but he certainly knew the true situation before dawn on the following day.

SEVEN

THE FALL OF TOBRUK

_____

14 June

There was now no doubt in Ritchie's mind that it was impossible to stick to the decision he and Auchinleck had arrived at the day before, and that he had to act very quickly if 1st South African and 50th Divisions were not to be cut off. Ever since February it had been accepted that, if a withdrawal from the Gazala line was forced on him, the next stand should be made on the Egyptian frontier, and that Tobruk was not to be allowed to become 'invested'. 'Should this appear inevitable', had been Auchinleck's instruction, 'the place will be evacuated and the maximum destruction carried out in it, so as to make it useless to the enemy as a supply base. In this eventuality the enemy's advance will be stopped on the general line Sollum–Fort Maddalena–Jiarabub.'[1] Furthermore, as soon as he had returned to Cairo, Auchinleck had written a letter to Ritchie, forwarding outline contingency plans to meet 'the worst possible case, which is the defeat of your army and the consequent need for holding the frontier position',[2] although this did not reach Ritchie until after he had given the order to Gott to withdraw his two forward divisions to the frontier, which he did at 0700 hrs on 14 June. The withdrawal was to take place that night, 1st South African Division by the coast road through Tobruk, covered by 1st Armoured Division, while 50th Division broke through the Italians facing them and drove through the desert in a wide sweep round south of Hacheim back to the frontier.

Unfortunately for Auchinleck, he had, on the previous day, informed London of his decision to 'stand and fight', and, early in the morning of the 14th, had received a reply from Churchill saying: 'Your decision to fight it out to the end most cordially endorsed. We shall sustain you whatever the result. Retreat will be fatal. This is a business not only of armour but of will-power. God bless you all.'[3] Will-power was not going to keep Gott's two divisions from being isolated. It was will-power that was needed to face hard realities and take unpleasant decisions, which would be highly unpopular with superiors.

Connell criticizes Ritchie for ordering the withdrawal 'in flat disregard of the orders which Auchinleck had given him the previous day, which had during the night received the full support of the Prime Minister, the CIGS and the War Cabinet';[4] but the situation had changed from that which they both believed had obtained when Auchinleck endorsed the decision recommended by Ritchie. They must have discussed alternatives, and we do not know whether or not they reviewed the pros and cons of a withdrawal to the Acroma–El Adem line, which Auchinleck was now to insist that Ritchie should hold. If neither raised the possibility, it was a serious omission. If such a withdrawal had been considered a possibility, Ritchie should at least have consulted Auchinleck about the destination of one or both of Gott's divisions, even if he could not wait for approval of the order to withdraw. If it had not been considered, or had been dismissed as an option, Auchinleck was at fault for imposing it on Ritchie without warning. The events which followed, and the exchange of messages between all levels, have been fully recorded in both the British and the South African Official Histories, which give a much clearer picture than Connell's prejudiced account, in which the dates of some of the signals are incorrect. There were misunderstandings, some of which were due to messages crossing each other, and to the changes in the situation by the time the reply had been received. Others arose out of the unwillingness of both Ritchie and Auchinleck to reverse attitudes they had already adopted. Both underestimated what Rommel could still achieve and overestimated what Ritchie could get his army to do.

In the signal which Ritchie sent to Auchinleck at 1030 hrs on 14 June, after a 'guarded and rather obscure' telephone conversation between 0900 and 0930 hrs,[5] he did not make it clear that he had ordered Gott's divisions back to the frontier, but 'into Army Reserve', and stated that he 'hoped initially to be able to stand on position Western perimeter Tobruk–El Adem–Belhamed with mobile forces operating from desert to the South'. He went on to say that, although he did not think that Rommel 'with his present strength' could 'closely invest' Tobruk, there was a risk that 'the back door could be closed'; that Tobruk had a month's supplies, and that he believed that 'we can restore the situation within that period and thereby save all the installations there'. He posed as alternatives 'to accept a risk of temporary investment in Tobruk, or to go whole Hog, give up Tobruk and withdraw to the frontier'; in other words he had no confidence in his ability to defend for long the initial stand he had described. Auchinleck sent a brief reply at 1215 hrs, received at Headquarters Eighth Army at 1307 hrs, saying: 'Even if you have to evacuate Gazala, you should hold Acroma, El Adem and to the south, while I build up reinforcements on the frontier . . . Are you able to do this?'[6] Before Ritchie had had an opportunity to answer that question, a much more definite order was despatched from GHQ which gave permission for the withdrawal of the two forward divisions 'if in your opinion the situation has so deteriorated that you can no longer leave [them] in main Gazala position without certain risk of their being cut off and isolated'. It then stressed that the enemy 'cannot really be in a position to carry out large-scale offensive operations for indefinite period at pace he has been doing', and that: 'This being so Tobruk must be held and the enemy must not be allowed to invest it. This means that Eighth Army must hold the line Acroma–El Adem and southwards and resist all attempts to pass it. Having reduced your front by evacuating Gazala and reorganized your forces, this should be feasible, and I order you to do it. If you feel you cannot accept the responsibility of holding this position you must say so.' A sharp change from 'Are you able to do this?'

This signal[7] arrived at Eighth Army at 1520 hrs. By the time it had been deciphered, Ritchie had left for Gott's and then Norrie's headquarters and, flying in a captured Fieseler-Storch light aircraft, did not get back until 1830 hrs, according to his ADC's diary of his movements,[8] although Playfair states that he did so at 1600 hrs.[9] Whichever it was, the time that had been fixed for the start of the withdrawal was 1800 hrs, and it was obviously too late and would cause intense confusion, to try and change the orders he had given that morning. There was considerable concern in any case as to whether the withdrawal would succeed. By midday Eighth Army had received ULTRA information that Rommel had ordered the Afrika Korps to drive north and cut the coast road,[10] and Gott had good reasons to doubt, knowing Pienaar, if he would obey an order to stop anywhere short of the frontier. Rommel's diary[11] confirms that Ritchie and Gott were right in their concern, and that the decision to withdraw was taken none too soon.

Ritchie rang GHQ at 1730 hrs (which favours Playfair's time of return) and spoke to Brigadier Davy, who had just returned from a visit to Eighth Army. He said that he accepted the task and would do his best, but that he could not guarantee to hold the line from Acroma to El Adem southwards. If he failed, and was compelled to withdraw to the frontier, he wished to accept the investment of Tobruk and again asked for the Commander-in-Chief's approval.[12] It is astonishing that, if Ritchie's critics are to be believed, GHQ still had no idea that Gott's two divisions had been ordered back to the frontier, when Davy had spent most of the day at Headquarters Eighth Army and had, to quote Playfair, 'the latest information'.

Auchinleck's second signal was followed by a formal operation order, despatched from Cairo at 2040 hrs local (not 1950 hrs as given by Connell). It was received at 2345 hrs, but, as there were errors in transmission, it could not be deciphered, and the full text was not cleared until 1335 hrs on 15 June. The signal difficulties may have been partly due to the fact that Ritchie's main headquarters was on the move back to near Sidi Barrani (see Map 2) during the night, his tactical headquarters remaining on the previous site of main near Gambut. The operation order concluded with the words:

To sum up:
    (a) The general line Acroma–El Adem–El Gubi to be denied to the enemy;
    (b) Our forces will NOT be invested in Tobruk and your army is to remain a mobile field army;
    (c) The enemy's forces are to be attacked and destroyed as soon as we have collected adequate forces for an offensive.[13]

This order had crossed a signal from Ritchie, replying to the earlier signal. It was originated at 2000 hrs and enlarged on his telephone call. It gave the reasons why he preferred the western perimeter of the Tobruk defences to Acroma. He said that he had contemplated establishing two brigade defensive positions east and south-east of El Adem,

... but these would be isolated and all of them including El Adem and El Gubi would be liable to destruction in detail by enemy forces unless we had armour in support. I consider that our experience so far has proved the truth of this and I realized that if ever we did withdraw to this line our armour would previously have been defeated and we would therefore NOT be able to provide the requisite armoured support for these localities. So I abandoned the idea as explained to the CGS when he was here.[14]

The reference to the CGS, Corbett, is mysterious, as there is no record of a visit by him since 7/8 June until the following day, 15 June, when he arrived at 1000 hrs and left at 1600 hrs, having seen Pienaar and Lumsden at Ritchie's tactical headquarters at Gambut while he was there.[15] In this signal, Ritchie explained that, although he was doing all he could to concentrate all the guns, field and anti-tank, motorized infantry and tanks under Messervy to operate on the southern flank, the reorganization involved would take 'a few days', and he could not guarantee that the enemy would allow him that time – a realistic assessment as it proved. If he did not have time to reorganize and Rommel

... gets astride the eastern heights from Tobruk, I will be faced with a decision to allow Tobruk to be invested or to order the garrison to fight its way out. The garrison probably could fight its way out, but it would undoubtedly lose a considerable amount of equipment and transport and arrive on the frontier in a disorganized condition. Having regard to resources of ammunition, food and water now in Tobruk and in ships in Tobruk, I feel confident that it could hold out for two months on its own resources [this was the advice he had received from Gott]. The policy which I recommend, therefore, with all my conviction is

(a) to fight alongside Tobruk to prevent it being invested;
(b) If I fail, to allow Tobruk to be invested rather than order the garrison to fight its way out in difficulties. If this is a correct interpretation of your signal, I accept responsibility.

Both Playfair and Connell omit the first part of this signal quoted, perhaps nonplussed by the reference to the CGS, which should have made clear that 1st South African and 50th Divisions were not intended to occupy positions in that area, although no specific reference was made to their destination. It seems incredible that Davy, having returned to GHQ, did not know this, whether or not the implication in this signal of Ritchie's was picked up by others at GHQ. It was in any case awkward that Churchill, late on 14 June, had signalled:

To what position does Ritchie want to withdraw the Gazala troops? Presume there is no question in any case of giving up Tobruk. As long as Tobruk is held no serious enemy advance into Egypt is possible. We went through all this in April 1941. Do not understand what you mean by withdrawing to 'old frontier'.[16]

It is not clear where Churchill had picked up 'withdrawing to the old frontier' – presumably from a report sent by GHQ to the War Office. Both Churchill's own account[17] and Connell[18] quote only the signal sent by Casey, Minister of State in the Middle East, on 14 June, in which he said: 'It has been agreed that Acroma–El Adem should be held and Auchinleck has sent Ritchie an order to that effect. The 1st South African and 50th Divisions are being withdrawn from the Gazala positions.' Nor is it clear what Auchinleck himself believed. What Ritchie intended is clearly revealed by his personal signal to Norrie, originated at 2030 hrs that evening:

Greatest danger present time is enemy investing TOBRUK. Main contribution which 30 Corps can make is in conjunction with 13 Corps to prevent enemy closing Eastern exits TOBRUK. Your role therefore is to deny enemy escarpment point 162 [immediately north of El Adem] to Belhamed [three miles north of Sidi Rezegh]. To do this necessary you will prevent enemy operating in area El Adem to Belhamed to Gubi and keep him as far West of this area as possible. I consider that enemy armour must be nearing exhaustion and may give us a few days respite during which I will do my utmost to strengthen you. You are NOT restricted in the use of such armour as may be allotted to you. Having regard to your resources a mobile policy will probably best achieve your object and an organization will be set up to enable all available columns with their gun power to be concentrated on a threatened area. Great sacrifices may have to be incurred to achieve this end on which 13 Corps are so dependent.

(This order was amended next day in a signal, which read:

Cancel last sentence but two dealing with use of armour and substitute quote our armour will be husbanded as a reserve of striking power and therefore should not engage enemy tanks unless surmise great advantage. Enemy tanks must be dealt with mainly by artillery unquote.)[19]

15 June

The story at this juncture becomes confused by Connell's placing the wrong dates on two significant signals. He gives the time and date of 0745 hrs 15 June to the following signal, which, from the copy in Ritchie's papers, both from its sequence (CS1266) and its date and time of origin, was clearly originated at GHQ at 0745 hrs *GMT* (1045 hrs local) *16* June, handed in at 1050 hrs and received at Headquarters Eighth Army at 1225 hrs, a timing accepted by the South African Official Historians.[20]

You have done well in getting 1 SA Div out so successfully and hope that you will be equally successful with 50 Div. Your army is now reasonably concentrated and it is most essential that you should use this advantage at once by bringing maximum force into play in El Adem area. Realize that troops must be tired and disorganized but the enemy is probably more so [he certainly was tired, but was not disorganized] and these considerations must NOT interfere with the concentration by you of all available force at the decisive spot which is El Adem in my opinion. I look to you to spare nothing to achieve this.[21]

Connell implied that it was despatched as a result of a long conference held at GHQ during the night 14/15 June and that 'Your army is now reasonably concentrated' meant that Auchinleck thought that the two infantry divisions were in the Tobruk–El Adem–Bir Gubi area. He also gives an obviously wrong date, 14 June, to the signal sent by Ritchie at 2340 hrs *15* June, in which he reported that 'Elements of 50th Division have arrived at Maddalena [on the frontier] and give as their impression that three-quarters of division is coming through. 1st S.A. Division has passed East of Gambut and is in good condition. Details in about two days.'[22]

At about 1135 hrs 15 June Auchinleck replied to Churchill:

Have ordered General Ritchie to deny to the enemy general line Acroma–El Adem–El Gubi. This does NOT mean that this can or should be held as a continuous fortified line but that the enemy is NOT to be allowed to establish himself east of it. The two divisions from Gazala will be available to help in this. Although I do NOT intend that Eighth Army should be besieged in Tobruk. I have NO intention whatever of giving up Tobruk. My orders to General Ritchie are:
    (a) to deny general line Acroma–El Adem–Bir Gubi to the enemy;
    (b) NOT to allow his forces to be invested in Tobruk;
    (c) To attack and harass the enemy whenever occasion offers. Meanwhile I propose to build up strong as possible reserve in Sollum–Maddalena area with object of launching counter-offensive as soon as possible.[23]

This message is not inconsistent with knowledge that the divisions had been withdrawn to the frontier, where they would be reorganized in order that they could then 'be available to help' in ensuring that 'the enemy was not allowed to establish himself east of the Tobruk–El Adem–Bir Gubi line' which was not to be 'held as a continuous fortified line'. If there was still a misunderstanding at GHQ on 15 June, it was dispelled by a situation report from Eighth Army, originated at 1405 hrs and received at 1650 hrs, which reported: 'Main body 1 SA Div reported 1015 hrs moving east from Tobruk to frontier area.'[24] The South African Official Historians[25] suggest that it was the mention of the frontier area in this report which provoked Auchinleck to send a MOST IMMEDIATE signal to Ritchie at 2345 hrs local, saying: 'I hope El Adem has successfully resisted attacks today. If El Adem still holds, its area should be reinforced without delay so as to ensure that Tobruk is defended without being invested. Grateful for early information of changes in situation at El Adem.' In any case, as has already been recorded, Auchinleck's CGS, Corbett, had flown up to Gambut that day and delivered to Ritchie a formal operation order, based on the conference held at GHQ during the night 14/15 June. Connell's account[26] states that Ritchie had 'declined to reinforce the area between Tobruk and El Gubi with static infantry in position, or to guarantee that he could prevent Rommel from moving further east'; that he had 'flatly refused to carry out his instructions, saying that they were no longer possible'; that 'we thumped the desk and shouted at each other', and that Corbett had returned that evening to Cairo (he left Gambut about 1600 hrs) deeply depressed. If that was the case, Auchinleck's signal was more likely to have been sparked off by Corbett's report, and both that signal and the 'You have done well' one, if its date of 16 June is correct, as it clearly seems to be, seem an inadequate reaction to Corbett's story.

16 June

Ritchie's signal (U1425) of 2340 hrs 15 June, referred to above, must have arrived at GHQ after Auchinleck had sent off his, and would have been on Auchinleck's desk first thing in the morning of 16 June, alongside one from Churchill, saying:

We are glad to have your assurance that there is no intention of giving up Tobruk. War Cabinet interpret your telegram to mean that, if need arises, General Ritchie would leave as many troops in Tobruk as are necessary to hold the place for certain.[27]

Before answering this awkward one, Auchinleck at last gave Ritchie an answer to his original question. Sent at 0800 hrs 16 June, it was:

Although I have made it clear to you that Tobruk must not be invested, I realize that its garrison may be isolated for short periods until our counter-offensive can be launched. With this possibility you are free to organize the garrison as you think best and to retain whatever administrative services and stocks of all sorts you consider necessary either for the service of the garrison or to assist the counter-offensive.[28]

At least that uncertainty was cleared away, and Ritchie knew that he did not have to plan for the withdrawal of Klopper's[29] 2nd South African Division and the additional troops he had placed under his command, nor for the evacuation or destruction of the stores inside the perimeter.

Auchinleck then went into a long conference with Casey and his fellow Commanders-in-Chief about how to answer Churchill's message. The result was signed at 1515 hrs and read:

War Cabinet interpretation is correct. General Ritchie is putting into Tobruk what he considers an adequate force to hold it even if it should become temporarily isolated by enemy. Basis of garrison is four brigade groups with adequate stock of ammunition, food, fuel and water. Basis of immediate future action by Eighth Army is to hold El Adem fortified area as pivot of manoeuvre and to use all available forces to prevent enemy establishing himself east of El Adem and Tobruk. Very definite orders have been issued to General Ritchie and I trust he will be able to give effect to them. Position is quite different from last year as *we* and *not* enemy now hold fortified position on frontier and can operate fighter aircraft over Tobruk even if use Gambut landing grounds should be temporarily denied to us. It seems to me that to invest Tobruk *and* to mask our forces in the frontier positions, the enemy would need more troops than our information shows him to have. This being so, we should be able to prevent the area between the Frontier and Tobruk passing under enemy control. I have discussed with Minister of State and other Cs-in-C who agree with the policy proposed.[30]

This signal reached Churchill shortly before he set off for a meeting with Roosevelt in Washington, and he sent a comforting reply, saying that he was thankful that Auchinleck 'had succeeded in regrouping Eighth Army on the new front in close contact with your reinforcements, and the Cabinet was very glad to know that you intended to hold Tobruk at all costs'. He went on to emphasize the superiority that armoured warfare conferred on the offensive over the defensive.[31]

The truth of that was being demonstrated by Rommel. On 15 June 90th Light Division had attacked 29th Indian Brigade's two battalion 'box' at El Adem without success, but 21st Panzer had overrun the isolated battalion position covering the pass where the Axis by-pass road crossed the escarpment three miles to the north-west. Both 29th and 20th Indian Brigades, (the latter holding a two-battalion position at Belhamed, with its third two miles to the south at Sidi Rezegh) were under the command of

Messervy, whose 4th Armoured Brigade was on the move south from Gambut; there it had spent the previous day trying to organize an effective fighting force out of the remnants of all the armoured regiments of both 1st and 7th Armoured Divisions. Norrie had ordered it to move south from Gambut on the 15th, but Richards protested and spent the night there, prepared to move south up the escarpment at 0800 hrs 16 June. On that day the attack on El Adem was renewed, while 21st Panzer by-passed it to the north, and, having been heavily bombed by the RAF, attacked the position at Sidi Rezegh at 1600 hrs, and Ariete held off columns from 7th Motor Brigade to the south. When both Indian Brigade commanders appealed to Messervy for help, he said that none was available, as 4th Armoured Brigade was still not ready for action. Its move south from Gambut had taken some time. Once south of the escarpment, the brigade had moved west until, as its war diary records,

the opening of the Sidi Rezegh gap was on our right flank [i.e. about eight miles southeast of Sidi Rezegh]. 40 enemy tanks had been reported in the area throughout the day and the Brigade Comd thought it was unwise to expose the tanks by advancing further to the west. The Brigade faced NORTH and took up a battle position facing this gap. At about 1800 hrs enemy tanks appeared and an engagement ensued.[32]

From the start Messervy had been anxious about the positions of these Indian brigades and, when he visited Brigadier Reid[33] at El Adem on the 15th, had told him to 'hold out as long as possible to give Tobruk time to settle in, but that he should withdraw before he should be so hemmed in as to make escape impossible.'[34] When Norrie discussed the situation with Ritchie on the evening of 15 June, they both agreed that El Adem could and must hold out, Ritchie promising to see what Gott could do to help by a westward attack next day. On 16 June, Messervy, giving his opinion that the garrison could last only another 24 hours at most, asked Norrie's permission to order withdrawal that night, for which he had made provisional arrangements; the request was referred to Ritchie, who at 1425 hrs refused and said that El Adem must hold at all costs.

At 1630 hrs Ritchie originated a signal to Auchinleck in which, having thanked the C-in-C for his permission to allow Tobruk to be 'temporarily isolated', he went on to say that, having discussed the matter at length with Gott, whose headquarters was now in Tobruk, he felt that

we can always accept investment for short periods with every prospect of success if we go all out to build up strength in south. Belhamed is the most vital place of all in ensuring keeping door open. So we must aim at holding El Adem to cover that place

... Am trying in accordance with your wish to reinforce El Adem box with additional artillery, but this has not yet been possible due to tactical situation here.

An hour later, Norrie, under renewed pressure from Messervy, no doubt provoked by the attack on Sidi Rezegh, discussed the situation with Ritchie again by radio. In view of all that has been written about Ritchie's surprising decision to leave the matter to Norrie's discretion, it is of interest to quote in full the record in the war diary of his tactical headquarters.[36]

1730 hrs 16 June. R/T conversation Comd 30 Corps–Army Cmd:
Cmd 30 Corps
1. Your wire received and quite clear. I have the strongest views about 29 Bde and have already expressed these to your BGS.
2. My columns continue their good work and have pushed further north; but they are still a long way from 29 Bde. I have already sent details of the bag which is up to the usual standard.
3. 4 Armd Bde is now approaching Sidi Rezegh. I hope things will be alright as he is well supported.
4. 20 Bde seems to be quite OK but the enemy is active in his area and digging in.
5. I would like you or BGS to read R.35 TOO 1450 from 7 Motor Brigade over ASC (Air Support Control) Tentacle. It explains more about my columns.
6. Would you thank RAF very much for their good work today.
Army Comd
My HQ is at Salum. The 29 Bde situation will be reviewed again. I quite understand your points. I have not heard the situation since this morning.
Comd 30 Corps
My columns are a long way from El Adem and are not doing what they did yesterday. There is definitely more shooting at El Adem. They are quite happy but it takes time to make arrangements for withdrawal and I would be grateful for an early decision.
Army Comd
I am most anxious that El Adem should remain in our possession but I cannot myself tell local situation and although I would like 29 Bde to remain, only you can see whether this is possible. How many days supplies have they?
Comd 30 Corps
Six days.
Army Comd
I consider I must leave this matter to you as the local situation must decide. But you must fully realize the importance of El Adem to us.

At 1900 hours, by which time the Sidi Rezegh position had been overrun, Messervy received from Norrie the permission he had been eagerly seeking; but when he spoke to Reid, the latter said he would prefer to wait another 24 hours. His troops were keyed up to resist and a hasty withdrawal at night could lead to confusion. Messervy reluctantly left the decision to him, saying that he should get out, if an opportunity occurred. At about midnight the brigade withdrew without interference from the enemy, but this was not realized at higher levels until much later. Eighth Army's midnight situation report to GHQ stated that '90th Light Division formed up to attack El Adem but nothing materialized' and Ritchie did not clearly understand the true situation until the following afternoon. At 0100 hrs 17 June he had another wireless conversation with Norrie, in which he said, 'Policy regarding Brigadier Reid and 20 Bde is the same. Therefore primary importance that 7 Armd Div does all it can to support them,' to which Norrie replied: 'Brig Reid reported not in position to withdraw tonight owing to change of order, but in accordance with our conversation this evening given discretion in matter ... Will continue follow orders but situation may now prevent any withdrawal by Brig Reid and 20 Brigade.' At 0700 hrs 30 Corps reported: '29 Bde believed OK. W/T not working. Heavy shelling El Adem during night. 29 Ind Bde may be in middle withdrawal. 4 Armd Bde k.o. 4 Mk III and 2 M13 last night now operating Sidi Rezegh area. 20 Bde holding present position anyhow unless forced withdraw.' It was not until 1150 hrs that Norrie, who was with Messervy, having visited Richards on the way, reported 'Brigadier Reid 29 Bde withdrew towards Bir El Gubi', but Ritchie did not seem to have finally hoisted it in until he had another radio conversation with Norrie at 1345 hrs 17 June.[37]

17 June

The troops under Norrie's command now left 'keeping the door open' consisted of 20th Indian Brigade's two-battalion position at Belhamed; 21st Indian Brigade and 2nd Free French Brigade 20 miles to the east on the escarpment south of Gambut; and 7th Armoured Division, with 7th and 3rd Indian Motor Brigades operating columns in the general area between Sidi Rezegh and Bir Gubi, and 4th Armoured Brigade. The last had about 90 tanks, which their crews were busy putting in order, although Norrie's orders had been that the brigade should 'dominate the Sidi Rezegh area'. On Messervy's orders Richards sent two columns, formed from his motor infantry battalion and artillery regiment, to help 20th Indian Brigade at Belhamed, which appeared to be the next target for the Afrika Korps. At 1400 hrs Messervy ordered Richards to move his tanks to the area between Sidi Rezegh and El Adem in order to attack the enemy threatening Belhamed in the flank. Richards, who knew the area well, protested that it was 'obviously unsuitable', presumably because, if his tanks were on top of the southern escarpment, they would be out of range of the enemy, and if they were below it, they could be overlooked from all sides – the reasons why his predecessor, Gatehouse, had been reluctant to move into the same area the previous December to rescue the New Zealand Division, which had then been occupying Belhamed. The brigade's war diary records:

They [HQ 7 Armd Div] replied that the Corps Comd [Norrie] was himself coming down to see the Bde. COs were called in to receive their orders and batteries were called in to refuel. At 1600 hrs the Bde Comd went to see the Corps Comd at SIDI MUFTAH [ten miles southeast of Sidi Rezegh]. At 1700 hrs there were reports of enemy tanks moving EAST along the Trigh Capuzzo on about the 450 grid [12 miles east of Sidi Rezegh, 6 miles south-west of Gambut].[38]

These tanks were in fact 15th and 21st Panzer Divisions, and the brigade moved to engage them, the regiments becoming engaged piecemeal and one hardly being involved at all. Two out of the three artillery batteries were still away with the columns. The battle lasted until dark, by which time another enemy force, said to be of 400 MT and 20 tanks, was reported moving southeast in rear of the brigade. Richards then withdrew all the way to the Trigh el Abd some 20 miles to the south, where he knew that he could replenish with fuel and ammunition. He reported that he had only 58 tanks left. Although the day's battle has been described as 'a terrific slogging match', particularly for the 9th Lancers, the actual tank casualties were only 9.[39] The reduction in tank strength from about 90 on 17 June to 58 on the 18th must therefore have been principally due to mechanical failure – proof that Richards was justified in wanting time for 'maintenance'.

At 2135 hrs 30 Corps reported to Eighth Army that Norrie had ordered 20th Indian Brigade to withdraw from Belhamed that night to the frontier. Many of them were captured on the way back, as Rommel had cut the coast road at Gambut at about midnight. The letter which Auchinleck had written to Ritchie that day, with its emphasis on continuing to attack the enemy 'who I am sure is exhausted and weakened, and would give anything for a period of rest and reorganization now' and 'has great anxiety over his fuel situation'[40] could not have been more inappropriate. It had crossed a signal which Ritchie had sent off at 1655 hrs, which said:

Communication 30 Corps very difficult owing to poor W/T conditions. Norrie was unable to reinforce El Adem and Belhamed yesterday. 29 Bde, less detachment B650, were withdrawn towards El Gubi last night as it was not possible to reinforce or support them before enemy could concentrate overwhelming strength of guns and armour against them ... orders for today. 7 Mot Bde to operate vigorously northward. 4 Armd Bde to dominate Sidi Rezegh area ... programme for forming columns between 18 and 21 June and two composite armoured regiments in one armd bde of 1 Armd Div ... All are in great heart and more than keen to be at it again. Morale throughout excellent. ... My intentions are whatever may happen to go on strengthening southern force with the object of operating offensively against his long southern flank which must be vulnerable. It may well prove that the correct place for this is well West of El Adem. Consider enemy's intentions either completely to invest and reduce TOBRUK or to mask TOBRUK and continue his advance. In either case in my opinion all my resources should be concentrated on offensive action against his southern flank. This of course will be combined with offensive against TOBRUK.[41]

It was, perhaps, receipt of this signal which sparked off Auchinleck's decision to fly up and see Ritchie next day.

18 June

As before, there is, tantalizingly, no record of what Auchinleck and Ritchie said to each other. Connell suggests that Ritchie was optimistic about his ability to prevent Tobruk being 'isolated' for long.[42] Ritchie's principal concern, urged on as he was no doubt by Auchinleck, was to build up a force capable of operating through the desert, and re-establishing a presence in the El Adem area, which would threaten Rommel's rear and join hands again with Tobruk, as Eighth Army had done in the previous November. If there was a difference between their points of view, it was probably that Auchinleck, as he was to indicate two days later, wanted to see this force produced as quickly as possible, while Ritchie, faced with the practical problems, wanted to make certain that the force would be effective and needed time to try and make it so. The practical result was the decision that Gott should assume responsibility for all the forces in the forward area, except Tobruk which came directly under Ritchie's command, while Norrie was sent back to Mersa Matruh to 'form and train a striking force with which, in due course, to resume the offensive'.[43] The mobile element of Gott's 13th Corps would be under command of 7th Armoured Division and consisted of 4th Armoured Brigade, with 66 tanks, 7th and 3rd Indian Motor Brigades, and one brigade each from 1st South African and 50th Divisions, all of them providing three columns each. The static element consisted of 10th Indian and the remainder of 1st South African and 50th Divisions, ordered to occupy a series of widely separated brigade positions stretching south from Fort Capuzzo.

19 June

Rommel spent 19 June making his final preparations for the assault on Tobruk, which was to follow almost precisely the plan he had intended to execute in November 1941, just as Eighth Army had attacked. Ritchie was in two minds as to whether Rommel intended this or to outflank the frontier positions. He sent a complicated order to Klopper in Tobruk, covering both contingencies; it told him, if Rommel attacked the frontier, to 'destroy enemy investing Tobruk', and gave two objectives, one two miles west and one six miles south-west of the perimeter, which, it was assumed, would achieve this.[44]

This order to Klopper to plan for offensive action outside the perimeter, combined with the prospect of co-operation from a relieving force operating in the general area of El Adem, complicated Klopper's plan for the defence of the fortress and distracted his attention, and that of his inexperienced and incompetent staff, from their priority task. When Gott, whose offer to stay in command of the garrison had been refused by Ritchie, handed over responsibility to Klopper on 16 June, he had told him to prepare three plans: one for defence; one for evacuation and one for counter-attack to recapture Belhamed, if it were lost. The Garrison consisted of Klopper's own two brigades, 4th and 6th; 11th Indian Brigade from 4th Indian Division; and, in reserve, 201st Guards Brigade, its three battalions being 3rd Coldstream Guards, 1st Sherwood Foresters and 1st Worcesters (the last in a poor state, having been pushed out of Acroma on 14 June with the loss of all their heavy weapons and personal belongings), and Willison's[45] 32nd Army Tank Brigade with 55 Valentines and Matildas and 20 more under repair. Artillery consisted of three field regiments and two additional batteries, and two medium regiments: 18 heavy 3.7in guns and the division's light anti-aircraft regiment of Bofors guns provided a rather thin anti-aircraft defence, and 69 anti-tank guns, including 16 six pounders with the Guards, an even thinner anti-tank defence for a perimeter of 30 miles, in which the average width of a battalion sector was 3 miles.

On 16 June, after a discussion with Klopper, Gott had told Ritchie that the defence was 'a tidy show' and better organized than it had been in April 1941, when the Australians had been besieged there (which in terms of numbers was true), and that it should be capable of holding out for several months. Klopper himself appeared confident, and in a letter of 16 June to Major General Theron, the South African Army representative at GHQ, wrote:

Things are going very well indeed with us here, as spirits are very high, and I do not think morale could be better under present circumstances. There is a general feeling of optimism, and I think there is every reason for it, although we expect to put up a strong and hard fight. . . . We are looking forward to a good stand, and we are supported by the very best of British troops.[46]

Willison, who had commanded the fortress reserve in the previous siege, was disturbed by this complacent attitude. He made a number of suggestions for a better organization of command of the reserve, for a reduction in the number of troops facing the sea, and for a co-ordinated artillery fire-plan, all of which were politely received, but not acted on. A strict rationing of artillery ammunition was imposed, which limited the use of it to interfere with enemy movement, which could be observed from within the perimeter.

20 June

At first light on 20 June Rommel attacked the sector in the south-east held by 11th Indian Brigade. At 0115 hours Ritchie had signalled Auchinleck:

There have been no signs today 19 June of enemy making any effort . . . to press eastwards towards the Frontier . . . I feel that . . . he is likely now to turn his main attention to Tobruk . . . we must be prepared for enemy undertaking main effort in either direction, and the best counter is to build up as strong a force as possible in the Desert to threaten his southern flank, while planning specific operations to be carried out by Tobruk garrison and 13th Corps to meet either eventuality . . . The building up of an adequate southern force is going to be a slow process.[47]

A rather different picture was painted in Eighth Army Intsum No. 238, covering the period 0800 hrs 18 to 0800 hrs 20 June: 'The latest indication is a WESTWARD movement from the GAMBUT area, and further SOUTH, which would suggest an investment of, or attack, on Tobruk in the near future, while our forces are to be held on the frontier by light element'; and the following day's summary recorded that: 'Throughout the afternoon and evening of 19 June ground and air report showed a steady movement of the enemy forces WEST from 48 grid line [12 miles east of Gambut].'[48]

At 0700 hrs the assault penetrated 11th Indian Brigade's defences, and, in response to an appeal by Anderson,[49] its commander, Klopper ordered Willison to send tanks to help him; but precious time was lost by the latter sending for the commanding officer to give him his orders, and it was not until 0930 hrs that the tanks reached 11th Brigade's area, where they failed to make contact with the infantry. From then on, the plans to give support to the brigade, and to employ the reserve infantry brigade in co-operation with the tanks, were a hopeless muddle, infantry and tanks being separately committed in driblets. It is not surprising that by midday most of Rommel's 113 tanks had penetrated well within the perimeter, heading for the harbour. The seriousness of the situation was not realized at Klopper's headquarters or at Eighth Army for several hours. At 1000 hrs Klopper's headquarters had reported: 'Enemy attacking SE area after aircraft attack advanced one mile. Counter-attack proceeding. RAF asking TOBRUK for best concentration and putting Bostons onto it.' This was received at 1045 hrs, at the same time as one from Auchinleck, alerted by ULTRA, saying: 'Enemy movement yesterday showed intention launch early attack Tobruk from east.' (It was originated at 0945 hrs, not 0630 as Connell, who fails to differentiate between GMT and local time, states.)[50] It went on: 'Know you realize extreme urgency interfering with this every means in your power and that you will act accordingly.' It was followed up by another: 'Am perturbed by apparently deliberate nature of your preparations though I realize difficulties. Crisis may arise in matter of hours, not days, and you must therefore put in everything you can raise.' Subsequent signals from 2nd South African Division were subject to much greater delay, the first indication that the situation was serious being a signal originated at 1345 hrs, received at 1430, briefly reporting that 40 tanks were now inside the perimeter. Earlier situation reports, which did not describe the situation as serious, were subject to long delay, that giving the situation at 1005 hrs not received until 1630, and one originated at 1255 hrs at the same time.

At 1625 hrs a report was received through the Air Support Control net, originated at 1550 hrs, saying: 'Approx 60 enemy tanks 415426 [the junction of the roads from Gambut and El Adem, known as King's Cross, nearly halfway between the perimeter and the harbour].' This was intended to be a personal message from Klopper to Ritchie, who had just left for Gott's headquarters near Sollum to confer with him and Norrie. He had left his main headquarters near Sidi Barrani with Whiteley at 1100 hrs to confer with them, but had returned when he received news of the attack on Tobruk. Before he left in the afternoon, he had drafted a signal to Klopper, signed for him at 1635 hrs by Major Ian Freeland[51] which clearly reveals the unreal atmosphere at Eighth Army headquarters at that time.

MOST SECRET and PERSONAL for General KLOPPER from Army Comd. Your 0/388 of 19/6. Well done ACROMA KEEP has made history. Quite agree with decision to evacuate. MAINWARING goes in to you tonight with plans etc [for operations outside the perimeter]. You are having a very tough fight today and I see this afternoon some enemy tanks have got through the outer perimeter. But I feel confident of your ability to put them out after destroying as many as possible. I am doing all I can to relieve pressure on you and our power to help you from outside will increase daily. The turn of the tide will come and feel quite sure of inflicting a crushing defeat on the enemy. I hope shortly to be able to provide sufficient ground security for R.A.F. to operate from L.Gs. nearer you and so increase their support for your defence. I will see about THOMPSON becoming Dy Comd TOBFORT. All good fortune to you personally and the whole of your grand command.[52]

It is doubtful if this was ever received by Klopper's headquarters; it was perhaps just as well not received, for at the time it was signed Rommel's tanks were three miles beyond King's Cross, overlooking the harbour only two miles away, and as shells began to fall about his headquarters and tanks were seen nearby, Klopper ordered the destruction of documents and signal equipment, and the dispersal of personnel. He himself later made his way to 6th Brigade headquarters in the north-west corner of the fortress, arriving there about 1830 hrs after dark. From that moment all command arrangements broke down, as they did within 4th Brigade, which had not been attacked, when the brigadier moved his headquarters at the same time.

If Headquarters Eighth Army was completely out of the picture, it is not surprising that the same applied to GHQ. A personal signal from Auchinleck to Ritchie, originated at 1756 hrs and received at 2120 hrs, stated: 'I feel strongly that enemy intends to attack Tobruk at once if he has not already done so', and then gave 'probable enemy dispositions' clearly provided by ULTRA. He continued: 'Vital ground to enemy is Sidi Rezegh–Ed Duda–El Adem but enemy do not seem to be strong enough to hold this ground against 8th Army while simultaneously attacking Tobruk.' He then proposed an ambitious and, in the circumstances, totally impractical major counterstroke by Eighth Army, 'to draw off Ariete Div and compel the enemy to use German troops to meet your advance'. He concluded with the sentence: 'I repeat that the enemy must not be allowed to launch an unimpeded attack on Tobruk.'[53]

A series of signals, with varying delays in transmission, only served to confuse the picture, the most reliable being that from the Senior Naval Officer Inshore Squadron, originated at 1745 hrs, received at 1945 hrs, which reported: 'Main position intact but enemy tanks supported by small party infantry approaching town. May be ordered to blow demolition any time. If so intend withdraw naval personnel and craft.'[54] The situation at nightfall was that Rommel's troops had driven a narrow wedge into the fortress, with its apex at the harbour, and in doing so had knocked out all Willison's tanks and put out of action two battalions of 11th Indian and one of the Guards Brigade, but also the latter's headquarters. Neither of the South African brigades, nor the Gurkha battalion on the coast north of the thrust, had been seriously involved, and the majority of the artillery, including one medium regiment, was intact; but Klopper, in spite of what he reported, took no steps to organize a counter-attack by night, to which the Afrika Korps, short of infantry, would have been very vulnerable. Having dispersed his headquarters, he would have had difficulty in organizing it. He decided that his situation was hopeless, issued a warning order to all units to prepare for a mass breakout at 2200 hrs and sent a message to Eighth Army, to which a set had been opened (or possibly kept open) at 2008 hrs: 'My HQ surrounded. Infantry on perimeter fighting hard. Am holding out but I do not know for how long.' At about 2100 hrs Whiteley got on the radio to Klopper and asked if the situation was in hand. The answer was: 'Situation not in hand.

Counterattack with infantry battalion tonight. All my tanks gone. Half my guns gone. Do you think it advisable I battle through. If you are counter-attacking let me know.' After consulting Ritchie, Whiteley replied: 'Come out to-morrow night, preferably if not tonight. Centre line Medauar [the corner of the perimeter east of Acroma]–Knightsbridge–Maddalena. I will keep open gap Harmat [where 22nd Armd Brigade is shown on Map 5] – El Adem. Inform me time and selected route. To-morrow night preferred. Destruction petrol vital.' Klopper thereupon entered into a council of war with his South African subordinates, who were divided between attempting to break out and trying to make a stand in the western sector, and giving up. At 0200 hrs 21 June Klopper signalled: 'Am sending mobile troops out to-night. Not possible to hold to-morrow. Mobile troops nearly nought. Enemy captured vehicles. Will resist to last man and last round.'[55] Between then and about 0600 hrs he changed his mind about whether the casualties involved in further resistance would be justified, as it could have had little effect on the rest of Eighth Army.

Ritchie, at 2200 hrs, sent a brief 'Clear the Line' signal to Auchinleck reporting the situation that Klopper had described in his radio conversation with Whiteley and saying that he had authorized him to fight his way out 'as apparently he feels he cannot hold out'. Shortly after 0600 hrs 21 June he got in touch with Klopper on the wireless and said: 'Noted about mobile elements. In respect of remainder every day and hour of resistance materially assist our cause. I cannot tell tactical situation and must therefore leave you to act on your own judgement regarding capitulation. Report if you can extent to which destruction POL[56] effected.' Klopper's despairing response was: 'Situation shambles. Terrible casualties would result. Am doing the worst. Petrol destroyed.' Ritchie closed the exchange with an embarrassing message of fulsome praise.[57] Klopper immediately set about arranging a surrender, which totalled 33,000 men, over half of whom were British, 2000 serviceable vehicles, 5000 tons of food and 1400 tons of petrol. German casualties are not known, but were undoubtedly light, although, when Rommel crossed the frontier on 22 June, the Afrika Korps had only 44 tanks. The only organized party to escape was led by Major Sainthill of the Coldstream Guards with 199 men of his own battalion and 188 from other units, following the recommended route. The 2/7 Gurkhas, on the left of 11th Brigade, went on fighting until last light on the 21st and the Camerons on the right until the morning of the 22nd, when they were threatened with extermination if they did not give up.

Could Ritchie have done more than he did to interfere with Rommel's attack and help Klopper? The quickest form of effort to apply was air attack;

but, with the withdrawal from the airfields round Gambut, the nearest group was round Mersa Matruh, nearly 200 miles further east. From there the 22 squadrons of fighters and fighter-bombers could not reach Tobruk: only the two squadrons of Bostons, one of Baltimores and one of ancient Blenheims could reach the area, although the South African Official Historians suggest that one squadron of Hurricanes with long-range tanks was available.[58] It was probably the escort to the Bostons, which bombed the area south-east of the fortress at 1320 hrs and again after dark, apparently without any significant effect on Rommel's operations.

At about midday Ritchie told Gott to order Renton[59] to move 7th Armoured Division to attack the enemy in the Sidi Rezegh area. At that time the division had a large number of columns deployed, operating northwards between the frontier and Bir Gubi, the nearest to Sidi Rezegh being two columns of 7th Motor Brigade. The division's war diary records: '7 Mot Bde were ordered to bring max pressure to bear on enemy from the rear in El Adem area, which was done.'[60] They were held off without difficulty by a German reconnaissance unit and the protective squadron for Rommel's headquarters (he, characteristically, was with the attacking troops), before they got near the Italian Pavia Infantry and Littorio Armoured divisions, which were protecting the rear of the attack in the El Adem–Sidi Rezegh area.[61] Fourth Armoured Brigade was on the move *eastwards* from the area to which it had withdrawn after its defeat on 17 June. The brigade had spent the previous two days reorganizing, as it received replacement tanks and personnel. On 19 June it had received a warning order to move south-east, but no executive order was received until after Gott had visited both the brigade and the divisional headquarters in the evening. Richards was then ordered to move his brigade at first light 20 June to Khireigat (see Map 2), 12 miles east of the frontier. They arrived there at midday, where, their war diary records: 'A rep of 8th Army arrived in the afternoon and was given a picture of the bde strength and then left to inform the Army Comd.'[62] It is not therefore surprising that 7th Armoured Division's activities were hardly noticed by Rommel. The sad fact was that Auchinleck and Ritchie could take determined decisions and order impressive-sounding moves, but neither the force nor the will existed at lower levels to put their resolutions into effect, and it was unrealistic of both of them, and of the staffs who advised them, to suppose that they would.

21 June

A sense of realism now began to affect both Eighth Army and GHQ. On 21 June, not yet aware that Tobruk had finally surrendered but expecting that it would do so, the Commanders-in-Chief Middle East considered a signal from Ritchie, sent from Gott's headquarters at 2359 hrs 20 June, saying that he believed that withdrawal to Mersa Matruh, fighting a delaying action to hold Rommel off, was preferable to trying to stand on the frontier, the defences of which could be by-passed, unless a stronger armoured force than was available to him could operate on the southern flank.[63] Although the Cs-in-C agreed with this view, there is a conflict between the account given by Connell, which for once favours Ritchie in saying that Auchinleck agreed with him, and that of the South African Official Historians who point out that, in his official despatch, Auchinleck wrote that, when he visited Ritchie on 22 June, he

was by no means happy at the decision to fall back on Matruh, perceiving that the reasons which had led to the evacuation of the frontier were equally valid in the case of Matruh ... Since General Ritchie alone was in a position to know whether the situation made it imperative to withdraw, I was obliged to leave him to make the decision. But I warned him that I did not consider Matruh to be more easily defensive.[64]

If he really did give him such a warning, and was not just being wise after the event, he was going back on the recommendation of the Cs-in-C's Committee of the previous day, perhaps in reaction to the reply which had been received from London. That stated:

The War Cabinet have carefully considered your telegram of June 21 and approve the general policy outlined. They feel, however, that sufficient emphasis has not been placed on the difficulties which confront the enemy in staging a successful attack on the Frontier defences [all Rommel had to do was to by-pass them]. If the fighting on the Frontier is to be merely a rearguard action, we feel that Matruh position may be quickly overrun, but if a resolute and determined defence is offered by the troops detailed for frontier defence, you may arrest his advance altogether, or at the worst gain time to build up an armoured striking force to operate offensively from Matruh.[65]

22 June

A resolute and determined defence was not by then on the cards, as Auchinleck discovered when he arrived at Ritchie's headquarters on 22 June. Pienaar had virtually refused to occupy the position known as The Kennels, 35 miles south of the Sollum–Sidi Omar defences, the latter held by Rees's[66] 10th Indian Division, the only force between them being the depleted 7th Armoured Division. Fiftieth Division was in reserve below the escarpment. With some justification, Rees had protested to Gott that the battered formations, which composed his division, would not be able to hold the enemy up for long, even if they were not by-passed, for which he was promptly sacked on 21 June. Auchinleck approved Ritchie's plan, which was that Freyberg's New Zealand Division, on its way from Syria, reinforced with a brigade from 5th Indian, would occupy Matruh itself, with 50th Division on its left on the escarpment outside the defences – 10th Indian would be behind it on the coast; all three would be under Holmes's[67] 10th Corps, whose headquarters was also on the move from Syria. Norrie's 30 Corps headquarters had already been sent back to organize the defences at El Alamein with 1st South African Division, and to begin reforming an armoured striking force. Gott would delay any enemy advance beyond the frontier. Auchinleck signalled Corbett that he was 'satisfied the situation is well in hand and all necessary action is being made to meet eventualities' and that Gott had 'orders to impose maximum delay on enemy'.[68] His chances of doing so were slender. The British Official History states that 'the plan which emerged [from the meeting of the Commanders-in-Chief on 21 June] was for a strong force under Lieut-General Gott to delay the enemy in order to gain time. This would enable the RAF to continue its attacks from landing-grounds as far west as possible and would cover the destruction of stores – in particular petrol and ammunition – that could not be got away.'[69] The only force available to Gott was 7th Armoured Division, which consisted of 4th Armoured Brigade, with two regiments, and the resuscitated 22nd with one, probably about 100 tanks in all, 7th and 3rd Indian Motor Brigades and several armoured-car regiments. Seventh Armoured Division's tanks represented the only armoured force Ritchie had left, and Gott's chances of delaying the enemy were severely reduced when the division was ordered, on the evening of 23 June, to move directly to Mersa Matruh.[70] Whether or not Ritchie had approved or initiated that order is not recorded; but a signal from Auchinleck, originated at 1600 hrs 23 June, queried the use of 4th Armoured Brigade with Gott's covering force. It read:

Understand value Stuarts as stiffening for motorized troops but are Grants and Crusaders or Valentines suitable for this kind of fighting? They are not numerous enough to engage enemy armour with success and medium tanks are unsuitable for delaying actions. Is it your intention to keep them forward and if so for what object or are you going to withdraw them to help build up strong armoured force at Matruh? I am strongly in favour of withdrawal once covering troops are on a mobile basis. 7th Armoured Division could continue control motor brigade groups until it takes over whole force from 13 Corps.[71]

If Ritchie did authorize the brigade's withdrawal, he would therefore have had the C-in-C's approval.

23 June

On that very evening Rommel's whole mobile force, but with only 44 German and 14 Italian tanks, reached the frontier wire. Ritchie sent a complacent signal to GHQ that evening. Although he appreciated that Rommel's aim was to cut off the frontier positions, and that he might 'develop this thrust in moonlight to-night', he made out that 7th Armoured Division had been successful in delaying Rommel's advance to the frontier and said that Gott was 'fully alive to the fact offensive action, especially after dark' against the southern flank of any such threat may have great effect.[72]

24 June

There is no record of such action being either planned or implemented. Rommel resumed his advance next day and met little opposition. By the end of the day, 24 June, he had reached the coast between Sidi Barrani and Matruh, Gott having successfully extricated 10th Indian Division from the Sollum defences before the coast road was cut. Rommel's achievement was remarkable, as the descent of the escarpment and the 'going' north of it was nbt easy. In that area, at Sofafi, 3rd Indian Motor Brigade got entangled in some old minefields and was roughly handled by 90th Light Division.

25 June

By the evening of 25 June Rommel's forward troops, in spite of difficulties with their fuel supplies, were in contact with the hastily occupied defences of Matruh. On that day, after Auchinleck and Dorman-Smith had treated themselves to a 'magnificent' lunch at the Mohammed Ali club in Cairo,[73] they flew to Bagush, east of Matruh, to which Ritchie had moved his headquarters, where Auchinleck announced that he was taking over personal command of Eighth Army himself. Shortly before midnight, he announced to his corps commanders that he 'no longer intended to fight a decisive action at Matruh and Sidi Hamza', but that 'the enemy was to be fought over the large area between the meridian of Matruh and the El Alamein Gap': that his aim was

to keep all troops fluid and mobile, and strike at [the] enemy from all sides. Armour not to be committed unless very favourable opportunity presents itself. At all costs and even if ground has to be given up [I] intend to keep 8th Army in being and to give no hostage to fortune in shape of immobile troops holding localities which can easily be isolated.

To this end every infantry division was to reorganize itself into battle-groups. Playfair's apt comment was:

Whether the fluid tactics were appropriate to the occasion or not, they were certainly new and entirely unpractised. The British tactical doctrine for a withdrawal had for many years insisted that anything in the nature of a running fight must be avoided. Thus the 8th Army was facing a bewildering number of changes. Its Commander had been replaced; it was retreating before a thrusting enemy; it had barely prepared itself for one kind of battle when it was ordered to fight another; and in the midst of all this it was told to change its organization and its tactics. But before anything could be done in the way of reorganization, the enemy put an end to one uncertainty by starting to attack.[74]

FIRST AND SECOND ALAMEIN

Auchinleck's declared intention to 'keep all troops fluid and mobile' was to have unfortunate consequences in the first few days after he had assumed direct command. Tenth Corps had under command 10th Indian Division, manning the old, delapidated, unmined defences of Matruh, and 50th Division, which had only two weak brigades, outside the defences to the east. Thirteenth Corps had 1st Armoured Division, which had taken over all the tanks of the 7th, above the southern escarpment 25 miles south-west of Matruh, and, 15 miles to the east, Freyberg's New Zealand Division, whose two brigades were in a position facing north on the escarpment at Minqar Qaim. Between these two divisions and those of 10th Corps, 5th Indian Division operated a number of mobile columns.

Rommel's plan was rash in the extreme. In the whole of the Afrika Korps, including 90th Light Division, he had only 60 tanks (of which about a third were light or command tanks) and not more than 2500 infantrymen. The Italians, following along behind, had 70 tanks and 6000 infantrymen. His plan was to drive Gott's armour away and encircle the defences of Matruh. He should never have succeeded. Closing up to Eighth Army's forward troops on 26 June, he thrust 21st Panzer and 90th Light next day between 10th and 13th Corps, while 15th Panzer advanced directly towards 1st Armoured Division. The former thrust caused some losses to both the 50th and the New Zealand Divisions and some confusion to the latter, much of their transport being dispersed. Lumsden held 15th Panzer's advance without much difficulty; and, when 21st Panzer attacked the New Zealanders in the afternoon, that was also held, although the divisional headquarters was heavily shelled, Freyberg himself being wounded.

Unfortunately, as a result of Auchinleck's new policy, everybody assumed that withdrawal was planned. Gott had issued contingency plans for this early in the day, and Auchinleck issued his at 1120 hrs. An hour later, after he had visited Freyberg, Gott told Eighth Army that he had given the latter permission to 'side-step if necessary'. At about 1700 hrs, just as Freyberg was

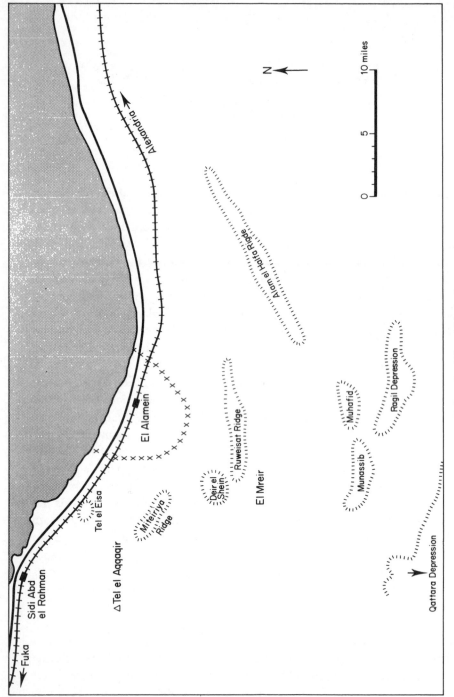

Map 6 First Alamein

wounded, messages appear to have reached each of Gott's divisions saying that the other had decided to withdraw, and that the commander of the one addressed could do so at his discretion. At 1930 hrs 13th Corps issued orders to start the first stage of withdrawal to Fuka, reporting the action to Auchinleck and repeating it to Holmes, who was planning a southward thrust to take pressure off Gott. Auchinleck accepted Gott's decision, but was unable to pass orders to Holmes to call off his attack and start withdrawal, as 10th Corps was out of touch with Headquarters Eighth Army from 1930 hrs 27 to 0430 hrs 28 June. Auchinleck only had the vaguest idea of what was actually happening, and it was not until the afternoon of the 28th that he realized that Rommel had cut the road between Matruh and Fuka. He rejected Holmes's suggestion that he should 'fight his way out' with the message: 'No question of fighting it out. No time to stage deliberate attack along road for which there is probably no objective. You will slip out to-night with whole force on broad front, turn east on high ground and rally El Daba. 13 Corps will cover you.'[1] 13th Corps did not get the order to do so until it was too late to implement. Once more, with a greatly inferior force, under frequent air attack and operating on a logistic shoe-string, Rommel had routed a force, superior in numbers of tanks, artillery and infantry. Command in Eighth Army had been totally ineffective, and practically broke down as, intermingled with Rommel's advancing troops, Auchinleck's divisions straggled back to the El Alamein line, which Norrie had been trying to organize, based on the position held by 1st South African Division astride the coast road. Rommel had in fact been in a very critical and dangerous situation. If, instead of a precipitate and ill-organized withdrawal, Eighth Army had delivered a resolute and properly organized counter-attack either on 27 or 28 June, the subsequent battles on the El Alamein line might never have been necessary. Both Auchinleck and Gott must bear a heavy load of blame for that, and Lumsden and Inglis, who took over command when Freyberg was wounded, must share some of it for being so anxious to withdraw quickly.

The subsequent events of the month of July 1942 are hailed by Auchinleck's admirers as his great victory and proof of his qualities as a commander. These, it is suggested, were the real turn of the tide, and doubt is cast on Montgomery's claim that his arrival in August, and his reorganization and revitalization of Eighth Army, culminating in the successful Battle of Alam Halfa in September, provided the climactic reversal of fortunes; it was Auchinleck, they assert, who had achieved that. It is not necessary to follow the ding-dong battles of that month, nor those that followed, in detail to arrive at a balanced judgement on that great historical controversy. Indeed, since it was initiated by Montgomery's unfair and tactless claims on assuming command, and developed in post-war writings, including notably Montgomery's memoirs and the retraction which he was forced to publish, the argument has cooled, and the protagonists on both sides have, to a degree, abandoned their more extreme claims and moved closer to a compromise position.

One of the most important sources, which has helped to bring this about, has been Professor Hinsley's magisterial second volume of the *Official History of British Intelligence in the Second World War*, which has already been referred to. That work makes abundantly clear what had hitherto been hinted at, but concealed under the cloak of official secrecy: that during this period Auchinleck was provided, both by ULTRA and by Army Y,[2] with very detailed and timely information of the state and disposition of Rommel's forces and of his intentions. It is not surprising therefore that his own general intentions were sound in concept. The problem lay in execution. This reliance on intelligence, based on wireless intercept, meant that Auchinleck's orders to his subordinates, still Norrie (until 8 July) and Gott, often demanded action at very short notice. Although new, fresh troops were introduced, the burden of action fell on those who had been through the depressing and exhausting period since 27 May. (The author, as GSO2 (operations) on Norrie's headquarters, calculated that from then until 1 July he had averaged $2\frac{1}{2}$ hours sleep in 24.) Others, like the New Zealanders, who had only entered the fray in the closing stages, were affected by a cynicism both about orders from above and about the possibility of effective co-operation with tanks, which were all manned by troops from the United Kingdom. This tendency to demand instant action, which was strongly encouraged by his mercurial 'chief of staff in the field', Dorman-Smith, was, in the opinion of the Brigadier General Staff, de Guingand, whom he had also brought with him from GHQ, an error.

Rommel's now exhausted and attenuated forces made contact with the northern end of the so-called El Alamein line – in fact three widely separated defensive positions, one held by 1st South African Division at El Alamein itself, one by a brigade of the New Zealand Division 15 miles to the south-west, and one by a brigade of 5th Indian Division 15 miles further to the south-west – on 30 June, arriving at the same time as 1st Armoured Division straggled in. Fortunately Norrie had gripped the situation. Not only did his staff set up a series of control posts which sorted out stragglers and directed them to appropriate destinations, but he had also persuaded Pienaar to provide a mobile force to operate outside the defences, and established in a position south of them 18th Indian Infantry Brigade; this had been hastily summoned from Iraq, commanded by a lieutenant-colonel and provided with a scratch field-artillery regiment, composed of batteries of three different regiments, and 9 Matilda tanks with crews scraped together from a reinforcement unit. Rommel's attempt to repeat in almost exact detail his envelopment of Matruh ran head-on into this brigade, which consisted of one battalion of the Essex Regiment, one of Sikhs and one of Gurkhas. Their gallant resistance blunted it, and was instrumental in turning the tide.

Auchinleck at this time appears to have had doubts about his chances of holding Rommel at El Alamein. His intelligence staff had greatly over-estimated the latter's strength in tanks, putting it at 120 German and 100 Italian on 30 June, whereas Army Y intercepted the strength return of 21st Panzer on 1 July at 37 and of the 15th at 17. Auchinleck was determined to keep his army in being and give up ground rather then see it outmanoeuvred in the field. He gave orders for defences to be prepared on the edge of the Nile delta and for plans to be made for a move of GHQ to Palestine; and for a step-by-step withdrawal through Egypt, part of his remaining force defending the Suez canal, while the rest withdrew up the Nile. The Mediterranean Fleet had already left Alexandria and moved through the canal into the Red Sea.[3] In the event 30th Corps, anchoring its operations on the fixed defences of El Alamein and taking little account of the Auchinleck/Dorman-Smith concept of moving columns of artillery around under the personal control of corps commanders, frustrated Rommel's attempt to bounce his way past El Alamein as he had at Mersa Matruh. By 4 July Rommel realized he had failed, his exhausted troops reduced to a total strength of 26 tanks fit for battle.

Auchinleck, made fully aware of Rommel's precarious situation by ULTRA and Army Y, attempted a counterthrust by 13th Corps from the south; but it petered out in a series of ill-coordinated actions, none of which was made in sufficient strength. Auchinleck now decided to switch his effort to the north. Norrie had been succeeded in command of 30th Corps on 8 July by Ramsden, the pedestrian commander of 50th Division. It is not clear whether he was sacked or left at his own request. He told the author at the time that it was the latter. If that was the case, it was a shrewd move, as he was able to present his story of what went wrong to the authorities at home before others got their word in, and he was on good personal terms with Churchill. Morshead's 9th Australian Division had been brought up to replace 1st South African, the latter side-stepping to the south. The two together launched an attack from the El Alamein defences on 10 July. Rommel, scraping together every man, German and Italian, he could lay his hands on, managed to hold the attack, which petered out on 13 July.

Switching his point of main effort again, Auchinleck planned another thrust along the Ruweisat ridge on the boundary between the two corps, to be launched on the night of 14 July. The attempt by Gott's 13th Corps to co-ordinate the action of tanks of 1st Armoured Division and the New Zealand infantry was a conspicuous failure, leading to recrimination on both sides, reinforcing the New Zealand distrust of tank support which was not placed firmly under their command. By 17 July this also had failed, although it had inflicted considerable casualties on Rommel's forces, both German and Italian, the former down to 42 fit tanks and the Italians to 50.[4] At the same time (21 July) 1st Armoured Division had 172 tanks (61 Grants, 81 Crusaders and 31 Stuarts) and Eighth Army was reinforced by 23rd Armoured Brigade with three regiments of Valentines, which had disem-barked at Suez on 6 July and reached the forward area on the 17th.

Auchinleck, well informed of Rommel's weakness, but also warned that he was laying minefields,[5] decided that he must strike while the iron was hot, although 23rd Armoured Brigade had had no opportunity to accustom themselves to the desert. To make matters worse, both Lumsden and Briggs were wounded in an air attack on 18 July, and Gatehouse, who was forming 10th Armoured Division in the Delta, was brought up to command 1st Armoured Division, under whose command were placed all the tanks, 2nd, 22nd and 23rd Armoured Brigades. Auchinleck's plan was another thrust in the area of Ruweisat ridge, carried out by 13th Corps. Fifth Indian Division would advance westward along the ridge, supported by 23rd Armoured Brigade, while the New Zealand Division repeated its north-westerly thrust from the south to converge with it, supported by 2nd and 22nd Armoured Brigades. The combined thrust was aimed at the area of El Mreir, where it was known that the Afrika Korps was deployed, the concept being that, in its current weak state, the Korps could not hold such a concentration and that, once it had been destroyed, the rest of Rommel's forces could easily be dealt with. Thirtieth Corps was to attack in the north in the coastal sector. The New Zealand attack reached its objective, but Clifton's[6] 6th Brigade was heavily counter-attacked by 15th Panzer Division at dawn, before 2nd Armoured Brigade's tanks could reach it, and neither the New Zealanders nor 1st Armoured Division made any further progress. The attack further north fared no better. 161st Indian Brigade's night attack had not gone well, and minefield gaps had not been fully cleared. Gatehouse wished to postpone 23rd Armoured Brigade's advance until this had been done, but Gott, believing the area a mile further south to be free of mines, ordered it to go ahead there; but the message to change his centre-line never reached Brigadier Misa. The two regiments (40th and 46th Royal Tanks) drove forward into a minefield under heavy fire. Some reached the final objective, but, counter-attacked by 21st Panzer, were ordered to withdraw, 40 tanks having been destroyed and 47 badly damaged. The third regiment of the brigade (50th Royal Tanks) supported 24th Australian Brigade in the second phase of 9th Australian Division's attack from the western sector of the El Alamein defences. The first, an infantry night attack, had been successful, but 50th Royal Tanks failed to marry up with the infantry and lost 23 tanks. All three prongs of Auchinleck's attack had petered out without inflicting serious losses on Rommel's German and Italian divisions. He made one more attempt, transferring 1st Armoured Division (less 22nd Armoured Brigade) to 30th Corps for a thrust south of the salient created by the Australians, starting on 26 July. Although supported by well-concentrated artillery, the attack became confused among minefield gaps, delaying the advance of tanks to join the infantry of 69th and 24th Australian Brigades, who had penetrated beyond. The brigades suffered heavy casualties, and yet another attempt to defeat Rommel's inferior forces petered out.

Auchinleck now decided that further attempts with the same forces were not likely to succeed, and that a major reorganization of Eighth Army, placing tanks and infantry within the same divisions, would be needed before success could be expected. His signal to London of 31 July read:

An exhaustive conference on tactical situation held yesterday with corps commanders. Owing to lack of resources and enemy's effective consolidation of his positions we reluctantly concluded that in present circumstances it is not feasible to renew our efforts to break enemy front or turn his southern flank. It is unlikely that an opportunity will arise for resumption of offensive operations before mid-September. This depends on enemy's ability to build up his tank force. Temporarily therefore our policy will be defensive, including thorough preparations and consolidations in whole defensive area. In the meantime we shall seize at once any opportunity of taking the offensive suddenly and surprising the enemy.

When Churchill received this, the CIGS, Alan Brooke, was already on his way to Cairo, and Churchill decided to join him there. The results were Auchinleck's departure (accompanied by Corbett and Dorman-Smith, Ramsden to follow); the selection of Gott to command Eighth Army; Gott's death on his way back to Cairo, and the consequent appointment of Montgomery. Details of these events, and of the important battles of Alam Halfa and El Alamein, are fully covered in my book *El Alamein*. Comment will be restricted here to the major issues affected by material that has become available since that work was written.

First, the controversy over whether the plan for the successful Battle of Alam Halfa was a mere legacy from Auchinleck and Dorman-Smith.

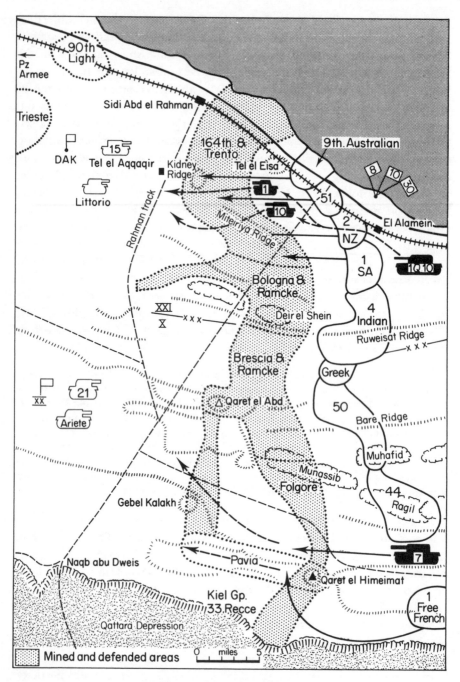

Map 7   Second Alamein

Montgomery was grossly unfair to his predecessor in telling Churchill, a few days after he had seized command of Eighth Army, that (to quote the words Churchill used in a signal to the War Cabinet from Cairo): 'It was intended in face of heavy attack to retire eastwards to the Delta. Many were looking over their shoulders to make sure of their seat in the lorry, and no plain plan of battle or dominating will-power had reached the units.' That was published in Volume IV of Churchill's *The Second World War* in 1951[8] and the accusation was repeated in Montgomery's *Memoirs* in 1958.[9] It was hotly contested by both Connell[10] and Barnett,[11] both of whom relied heavily on Dorman-Smith. In Barnett's commentary, inserted in the 1983 edition of *The Desert Generals*,[12] he comes closer to the line which emerges clearly from the evidence given by those officers at Headquarters Eighth Army, who had served Auchinleck and were taken on by Montgomery, quoted by Hamilton in the first volume of his official biography of the latter.[13] Barnett writes: 'Auchinleck had intended a mobile battle pivoting on the fixed defences.' The operation orders issued at the time (those of 30th Corps written by the author) make clear what these words were expected to mean: a collection of brigade 'boxes', based primarily on artillery, from which surplus infantry would be sent back to the Delta, disposed in depth between El Alamein and the Delta, between which mobile forces would operate against Rommel's incursion. In case that plan failed – as a good many people, including notably Freyberg, thought it would – troops were being held back in the Delta to defend it directly, in which event GHQ would move from Cairo to Palestine.

Montgomery's decisive contribution was to realize immediately that, if the 44th Division, held back for that purpose in the Delta, were sent up to reinforce Eighth Army, he would have enough troops to hold a continuous line of defence as far south as Alam Halfa. On that ridge, he would refuse his left flank, threatening any attempt by the enemy to turn it with counter-attack on the latter's left flank. All plans for manning reserve positions in depth at the expense of the front line, for sending back so-called surplus infantry, and for insuring against failure with contingency plans for withdrawal could be cancelled. It was very misleading for Barnett to write originally, and still to maintain, that the battle 'was fought on a plan conceived by Dorman-Smith, approved and initiated by Auchinleck, and from fixed defences largely dug before Montgomery left England'.

The next controversial issue is whether or not Montgomery could have finished off Rommel's Panzerarmee in that battle, thus avoiding the major subsequent Battle of El Alamein, the seven-and-a-half weeks which intervened between the two allowing the Germans and Italians to reinforce their forces, lay masses of mines and greatly improve their defences. There is a good deal of justification for that view. In my book *El Alamein* (as slightly amended in the 1979 edition) I wrote:

Could not Montgomery have delivered the *coup de grâce* at Alam Halfa? Theoretically it would seem that he might have done, and it is clear that at first he thought so too. If a swift riposte had been planned on the first day and rapidly executed, it might have succeeded; but the disappointing results of the action of 8th Armoured Brigade on the morning of September 1st, and of the New Zealand Division on the night of the 3rd, showed him only too clearly how blunt was the weapon in his hand when it came to attack. Montgomery was a realist, and there is no doubt that persistence in counterattack at that time would have gained him little and led to losses which he would regret later.[14]

Next, the Battle of El Alamein itself, the foundation of Montgomery's fame. Nothing that has been revealed in the last 25 years has caused me to revise the conclusions I reached then. They were:

There is no doubt that, of the true fighting strength of the divisions engaged, a very high proportion suffered casualties; but that is not to say that they were excessive by whatever standards that is judged, and certainly not so among the armour, either in terms of human casualties or of tanks knocked out; [and:] It is perfectly justifiable to maintain that tank losses could easily have been self-defeating, if the tanks had been made to do what undoubtedly Montgomery at first, and Freyberg all the time, wanted them to do; [and:] Criticism has been accentuated by the impression given by Montgomery himself that the whole battle went entirely according to plan. He is perfectly justified in maintaining that, in general terms, it did; [and:] It may have been expensive and unromantic, but it made certain of victory, and the certainty of victory at that time was all-important. Eighth Army had the resources to stand such a battle, while the Panzerarmee had not, and Montgomery had the determination, will-power and ruthlessness to see such a battle through. Just because the battle did *not* follow the course mapped for it, the organization of command soon became inappropriate. If Lumsden's 10th Corps had been right out on its own, well clear of the area captured by Leese's 30th Corps, it would have been perfectly suitable; but, as it was, the superimposition of one corps on another, and the duplication, confusion and opportunity for disagreement to which it gave rise, undoubtedly led to inefficiency and missed opportunities. Montgomery cannot escape blame for allowing this to continue beyond the time when it was no longer unavoidable, by leaving the New Zealand Division under Leese's command, although it was leading the pursuit after *Supercharge*.[15]

I now think that judgement errs on the side of being charitable. Montgomery made two fundamental errors. He arrived in Egypt imbued with a misconception of the part which the Afrika Korps had played in Rommel's Panzerarmee. It was not, as he imagined, a *corps de chasse*, but the principal fighting element of the army: the rest were little more than hangers-on. His second mistake was made when, on 6 October, he was forced to accept that his original plan was too optimistic, as far as the rôle of the armour was concerned, and it was changed to a less ambitious one. He should then have abandoned his idea of keeping 1st and 10th Armoured Divisions, with their three brigades of Sherman tanks, under Lumsden's 10th Corps. The best answer would have been to make Lumsden take over the southern sector, which included 7th Armoured Division, and divided the main assault area between Leese's 30th and Horrocks's 13th Corps. Far from being cautious, Montgomery was being too optimistic in expecting a breakthrough and pursuit at so early a stage of the battle.

Another basic mistake in the organization of command – a subject in which one would have expected Montgomery to be particularly expert – contributed a good deal to the failure of the immediate pursuit after the breakout at the end of the battle. Even if Freyberg's New Zealand Infantry Division had been a suitable formation to lead the pursuit – which it proved not to be – it was a major mistake to leave it under command of 30th Corps, with the three armoured divisions of 10th Corps sandwiched in between, undertaking too short a left hook. It aggravated the other mistake: trying, in a very confused situation at night, to get too many different formations out at the same time. Hamilton's second volume[16] throws some important new light on this phase of the battle, especially on the contribution to the confusion and delay made personally by Lumsden. As I made clear in *El Alamein*, Montgomery's claim that it was the rain, falling on 6 November, which prevented him from cutting off the remains of the Panzerarmee was not true. He had over-insured and paid for it.

Over-insurance was to be the keynote of the rest of the pursuit, until Tripoli was captured exactly three months after the start of El Alamein. As Montgomery wrote to Brigadier Simpson[17] at the War Office:

We have been to Benghazi several times before and have always had a disaster, which has negatived all the success gained ... I am determined that this time there will be NO setbacks, but it is hard work ... [followed by some rude remarks about staffs in Cairo, especially the air staff] ... I have now got to pause, to collect my scattered forces, and get my administration on a firm basis – it is stretched to breaking point at the moment.[18]

The Msus Stakes were not going to be run again.

With the capture of Tripoli, the Libyan desert campaign came to an end. Eighth Army's advance into Tunisia and participation in the final battles there belong to the story of Operation *Torch*, which began on 8 November 1942 with the Anglo-American landings in Algeria and Tunisia and ended with the surrender of the German and Italian forces in North Africa after the fall of Tunis in May 1943.

N I N E

WASH-UP

Wash-up is the British army's slang term for the conference after an exercise at which the commander, who has organized and controlled it, distills and discusses the lessons that are to be learned: the sordid chore that has to be faced after the stimulating meal. What would have been the main points of a wash-up after the Libyan desert campaign? Montgomery held just such a conference at Tripoli in February 1943, at which he pontificated about how to win battles. Its content is not worthy of much attention. Patton, who was present, is said to have remarked: 'I may be old: I may be stoopid; but it means nothing to me,' and Montgomery signally failed to follow the precepts he proclaimed in his next major battle, at Mareth.

One of the most recent, and most perceptive, historians of the British Army in the Second World War, General Sir David Fraser, has attributed the failures of Eighth Army in 1942 to lack of discipline at the top; to the slowness of the British; their failure to concentrate force at the crucial time and place: 'not a consequence of failure to understand the principles of war', but of 'failure to make the machine work'; the failure to impose, from the summit, a directing intelligence and will. He maintains that Rommel owed his success primarily to the fact that he was attacking.

This is not the least of the factors which led to a British military performance at Gazala inferior, in many ways, to that in *Crusader* six months before. To await the enemy's attack, to place troops in a purely reactive situation, to surrender the initiative is always to face a difficult task. It can lead to defeat – even defeat by smaller forces, provided that they are concentrated, well trained and led with the zest and energy which characterized the opponents of the British Army in the summer of 1942.[1]

From the preceding chapters it is clear that the key element of that criticism is 'failure to make the machine work', to which 'slowness' contributed a good deal. There was no lack of intention at the summit to impose 'a directing intelligence and will': the trouble was that it soon became dissipated as it descended the channel of command, partly, but not entirely, because the machine was not capable of producing the results demanded of it.

Was that the fault of the machine itself, or because those at the summit did not understand how the machine worked or of what it was capable? A bit of both. At the time, and since, blame has been attributed to different causes, depending on the viewpoint of the critic. The tank soldier tended to blame the technical inferiority (both in performance and in reliability) of his equipment; he blamed also the infantry for being unable to look after themselves and diverting him from his 'true' mobile rôle into one where he would be both more vulnerable and less effective (although his effectiveness in the mobile rôle after the Italian campaign was not apparent). The infantryman blamed the tanks for failing to co-operate with him closely when needed, both in attack and in defence, although an honourable exception was generally made for the 'I' tanks. The gunner laid much of the blame on failure to concentrate artillery fire, although the occasions when it would have been possible to effect a significant concentration, until the army itself was relatively concentrated back at El Alamein, were few and far between. The sappers complained that they were never called upon to help until too late, when there was insufficient time for them to make an effective contribution in constructing defences or in gapping the enemy's minefields. The more things went wrong, the more was everyone inclined to blame others. The parochial, tribal nature of both the British and the Indian armies, and the heterogeneous composition of Eighth Army, contributed significantly to this fissiparous tendency, particularly as both the high command and the tank arm were in the hands of men from the United Kingdom.

There were, therefore, to quote from the concluding chapter of my *Tobruk*, 'inherent deficiencies in organization, training and command which meant that the army's full power was never fully developed.'[2] That chapter deals fully with what I called the 'Bitter Lessons' of the *Crusader* and *Gazala* battles, and it would be a work of supererogation to repeat it here. The relative quality of the tanks on both sides was fully discussed, and the conclusion reached that it was not as significant a factor as was claimed at the time. Since then much has been made of the failure to concentrate the armour. That also needs qualification. It is ironic that in the battles in which Ritchie's armour suffered its heaviest defeat and after which superiority in tank numbers turned decisively in Rommel's favour – those of 12 and 13 June 1942 – the armour was all concentrated both in terms of space and of command. However it is clear that almost invariably it was locally dispersed, that is within the armoured brigades. Time and time again, individual regiments were engaged separately. The fault there lies not with the higher command, but at the brigade level. As has been already mentioned, 'tank experts' in Britain, notably Hobart, laid the blame on command being in the hands of officers who did not understand how to 'handle armour'; but in the Gazala battles all but one of the armoured and all the army tank brigades were commanded by officers of the Royal Tank Regiment: only 22nd Armoured Brigade was commanded by a cavalryman, and in *Crusader* the performance of Gatehouse certainly did not appear to be superior to that of Davy or Scott-Cockburn. The impression that Rommel's armour was always concentrated while the British were always dispersed is far from being a true picture. Rommel's two panzer divisions were often operating independently at a considerable distance from each other.

The problems of defence have already been discussed: the question of which areas to hold – how many, and in what strength (division, brigade or battalion); the need for all-round defence; what to do with the vulnerable vehicles; and, even if effective defensive positions were established, the fact that, if the mobile forces lost the battle, all of them could become hostages to fortune. Those problems were never satisfactorily solved, until Montgomery, on his arrival, realized that enough troops were available to hold a continuous line, as he had experienced it in France in the First World War. His successful defensive battle of Alam Halfa proved that defeat was not inevitable, even though the enemy had the initiative; but his attempt to counter-attack with the New Zealand Division was no more successful than any of Ritchie's or Auchinleck's attempts, and for the same reasons.

It was in attack that the German forces invariably proved more effective than the British. The reasons for this were varied, but chief among them undoubtedly was that they had effective standard methods combining the action of all arms, including most significantly the offensive use of anti-tank guns. The only tactical method of the same kind within Eighth Army was the classic 'set-piece' infantry attack, supported by 'I' tanks and artillery; and that often failed, even in 'Second Alamein', because of a breakdown in the intricate dove-tailing of action needed to ensure that the engineers had cleared gaps in minefields, captured by the infantry, rapidly enough for tanks to move through to support the infantry both in advancing further and against counter-attack by enemy tanks. Failure in the attacks on The Cauldron and in First Alamein was largely attributable to the fact that the tanks involved were from armoured brigades which not only had not been trained in the rôle of infantry support, but had an ingrained distaste for it. This had its origin partly in the pre-war fight to establish the tank as the primary fighting arm in its own right, and not just as an adjunct to infantry; partly in the attitude of the cavalry, who thought that the mobile rôle should be their privilege, relegating the Royal Tank Regiment to its original task of infantry support, an attitude accentuated by social snobbery; partly in that the tanks, with which the armoured brigades were initially equipped (the 'cruisers' with their thin armour) were clearly unsuitable for that rôle (the Grant however was originally designed as an infantry-support tank, its 75mm gun as a 'close-support' weapon); and, finally, one must admit, because infantry support was a rôle in which the chances of survival were significantly lower. It was not until after the end of the war that the distinction between the two different rôles of the tank was finally abandoned, although, both in Italy and in North-west Europe in 1944, brigades equipped with Sherman tanks, the successor to the Grant, including one commanded by the author (the 4th), alternated between both.

This factor plagued Montgomery during the Battle of El Alamein. His biographer is severe in his criticism of the armoured commanders, notably Lumsden and Gatehouse,[3] and there is no doubt that some of it is justified; but he fails to recognize the real problem faced by the tanks in attempting to emerge in broad daylight, in line ahead, from narrow gaps through the minefields in areas to which the enemy's attention had been concentrated by the artillery programme which had supported the infantry attack, artillery, much of which, until it were moved forward, could not reach out to deal with the anti-tank guns facing them. The fact that 22nd Armoured Brigade in 7th Armoured Division in 13th Corps at the south of the line, under commanders recognized as outstanding for their courage, vigour and skill – Roberts, Harding and Horrocks,[4] was no more successful, proves that the problem was not just a failure at the command level.

Was that failure as great, before Montgomery arrived, as so many critics, of both the pro-Montgomery and the pro-Auchinleck schools, have made out?

The British commanders were not supermen. They were neither better nor worse than those who succeeded them. They were faced with a form of warfare completely novel to all, for which their experience and training was of little value. As one who saw almost all of them at first hand and served under their successor (and under Ritchie again in North-west Europe), I am convinced that few of their successors would have achieved results much different. In the latter half of the war, intricate as the problems of planning might be, there was seldom, if ever, any danger of one's plans being completely disrupted by surprise enemy action. When mistakes were made, their results were less disastrous and far less obvious. If Montgomery had been appointed to command Eighth Army earlier, he would undoubtedly have refused to accept the anomalies of the situation in May 1942. Whether he would have solved them better, or been removed for protesting against them, is a matter of pure conjecture.[4]

A factor which is often glossed over is that of communications. Between the wars, the British army had been slow to adopt radio-telephony as its primary method of communication. The Royal Tank Corps had been pioneers in forcing the Royal Corps of Signals to introduce radio sets which could be used in a vehicle on the move. At the start of the war few infantry officers, certainly among the senior ones, had any experience of its use. Although the quantity and quality of radio sets gradually improved from 1940 to 1942, speech over distances of more than a few miles was often indistinct, and at night often impossible: always insecure. Resort to key and encipherment imposed significant delays. This inadequacy of radio communications, particularly between higher headquarters, was a major factor in the confusion which arose in the two 'Msus Stakes' of 1941 and February 1942. Another was the difficulty of movement about the desert, the surface of which was not the billiard table that some imagined. These problems became much simpler when the army was concentrated on a comparatively narrow front at El Alamein.

Messervy's unfortunate experiences in the Gazala battles illustrate the typical difficulties of a desert commander. When he stayed with his headquarters, it was overrun; when he left it, he was ignominiously forced to seek refuge down a well. Although the June days were long – far too long for the soldiers, whose only chance of rest was night – they could pass with little achieved. While commanders were on the move from one place to another and when they were in conference together, nothing happened. These periods absorbed long periods of the day, which appeared to pass somewhat in this manner:

First light: units break leaguer: armoured cars move out to locate the enemy. One or two hours pass before anybody has a clear idea of where the enemy are today. Divisional commanders visit brigade commanders to find out the form before returning to meet corps commander somewhere convenient to both. About two hours spent in travelling. Corps commander, who may or may not have seen army commander, confers with divisional commanders and probably gives orders. Probably nearly midday by now. No major change in dispositions made before this. Resulting from orders, armoured brigades may be moved to new areas, where divisional commander meets brigade commander and tells him what to do. More time spent in discussion. Brigade commander summons COs: orders issued, units briefed, etc. Probably about 4 p.m. or later by now. By the time that attack is launched, it is nearly last light and everybody realizes it cannot achieve much before dark, and so does not try very hard.

This may be exaggerated and a picture of the worst case, but it does represent the feeling one had at the time of how the day could slip past with nothing achieved. It was the price paid for surrender of the initiative, and it made it hard to regain it.[5]

What of the personalities involved? Now that they are all dead, I can write more frankly than I did over 20 years ago, when, as a serving officer, I was subject to the censorship of the War Office. I regarded Auchinleck and Montgomery with both admiration and affection. They were both inspiring characters in their own fashion. In retrospect, I believe that Auchinleck's chief fault lay in believing that morale was everything: that stirring phrases and ideas could win the day. He would have liked to have prepared Eighth Army as carefully for battle as Montgomery was able to do between Alam Halfa and El Alamein; but circumstances – events elsewhere and pressure from London to embark on an offensive – denied him that possibility.

My contacts with Norrie and Gott were much closer, and my admiration and affection for them, at the time, was even greater, especially for the latter. Norrie was a charmer, a most persuasive and likeable man, who was at his best in dealing with awkward characters; but there is no doubt – and I realized it at the time – that he was indecisive, and not firm enough with his subordinates. He was much too inclined to leave the decision to the man on the spot, and he tended to seek Gott's advice and to defer to it, before taking a definite line. This brought about the unfortunate situation in which Ritchie's two corps commanders appeared to be ganging up against him, which they often did because they felt that he was merely the mouthpiece of Auchinleck, far away in Cairo under the influence of the distrusted Dorman-Smith.

Gott remains the enigma. Almost all who served under him worshipped him: for his serenity, good humour and courage whatever the situation; but above all because whenever others were uncertain as to what to do, he was prepared to propose a positive solution, which, at the time, seemed wise. But the deeper one delves into the record, the more one understands why, from Gazala back to El Alamein, some of the Commonwealth commanders, Australian, New Zealand and South African, and their historians, have cast doubt on his judgement and exercise of command in that period, at the end of which he was undoubtedly exhausted. Tragic as it was for him, and all who loved and respected him, it was fortunate for Eighth Army that he did not assume command.

I have left Ritchie to the last, one of the aims of this book having been to defend the reputation which he himself refused to do. I served under him directly in North-west Europe, when he commanded 12th Corps, and came both to respect and to like him. He was a good, professional, straightforward soldier. If he had not been, Alanbrooke would not have thought highly of him as his Brigadier General Staff. There is no doubt in my mind that he never recovered from starting off on the wrong foot with Auchinleck – as a *chargé d'affaires*, not a plenipotentiary. His opportunity to remedy that state of affairs came after the clash with Godwin-Austen in the Msus Stakes of February 1942. It is now clear that it was Auchinleck's intervention that caused the counter-order which led to disorder. Ritchie should then have demanded either that he should be allowed freedom to command his army in his own way, or be replaced. But he was too decent, loyal and traditional a soldier to put his superior, whom he liked and admired, in such a difficult position. He was to suffer for it. High command in war demands tougher and more ruthless qualities; Montgomery knew this well and had no hesitation in employing them.

APPENDIX

General Sir Neil Ritchie GBE, KCB, DSO, MC

Neil Methuen Ritchie was born in British Guiana on 20 July 1897, the third child and second son of Dugald Ritchie, who was a successful sugar-planter there. However, a sugar-cane disease ruined his business, and he moved to Malaya, where he built up a successful rubber-growing business, retiring to England in 1917.

In 1906 Neil had left his parents in Malaya to attend preparatory schools at Eastbourne and Caterham before going to Lancing College in 1911. At the end of the summer term of 1914, he entered Sandhurst, his elder brother, Alan, having already joined the Argyll and Sutherland Highlanders. Alan suggested to Neil that he should apply for the Black Watch, into which he was commissioned on 14 December 1914. He joined its 1st Battalion in France in May 1915 and was slightly wounded in the hand at the Battle of Loos in September. When he recovered from that, he was posted to the 2nd Battalion in Mesopotamia.

The battalion, which had arrived there at a strength of 30 officers and 1011 men, had been reduced to one officer and 35, and amalgamated with a battalion of the Seaforth Highlanders. Ritchie became adjutant of the unit in June 1916, a month before the Black Watch battalion was re-formed, Ritchie remaining as adjutant until after Baghdad had been reached in March 1917. Here he developed paratyphoid and was evacuated to India, where he learned that he had been awarded the Distinguished Service Order. He rejoined the battalion, reassuming his post as adjutant, when it moved with the 7th Indian Division to take part in the final stages of Allenby's campaign in Palestine, where he was awarded the Military Cross.

After the war, he remained adjutant, Wavell for a time acting as commanding officer. In 1923 he joined the latter in the War Office as a GSO3, staying there until 1926, when he rejoined the 2nd Black Watch at Fort George in Scotland as a company commander. From 1928 to 1930 he attended the Staff College, where he was Captain of Cricket, and in 1931, as a major, joined 1st Battalion The Black Watch in India, but left them that year to take up the appointment of GSO2 (Training) at Headquarters Northern Command at Rawalpindi. It was in that post that he first met Auchinleck, then commanding the Peshawar Brigade on the North West Frontier, and was impressed.

Promoted Brevet-Lieutenant-Colonel in 1936, he was offered the post of military assistant to the Commander-in-Chief, General Cassels, but turned it down and took long leave, travelling leisurely eastward across the Pacific to North America. Friends in Canada suggested to this 39-year old bachelor that he should travel by New York to meet a Miss Minnes. Their match-making was instantly successful, a lightning courtship leading to engagement. But Ritchie's leave was running out, and he joined the 2nd Black Watch in the Sudan as a company commander in May.

This was a period when promotion to command in regiments like his was desperately slow, being ruled by seniority, and brevet-lieutenant-colonels, like himself, were offered 'accelerated promotion' into other regiments, where there were fewer majors recommended for command. Ritchie was transferred in this way to command a battalion of the King's Own, a Lancashire regiment, a few weeks after he and Sunny Minnes were married in London in December 1937. In September 1938 he took the battalion to Palestine, where, based in Jerusalem, he was under O'Connor's command. He left the battalion in the summer of 1939 on promotion to Colonel as instructor at the Senior Officers' School at Sheerness, but was almost immediately promoted again to become Brigadier General Staff to 2nd Corps, commanded by Alanbrooke, and went with them to France in the British Expeditionary Force, commanded by Gort.

After Dunkirk and the later evacuation from Cherbourg, Ritchie, promoted Major-General, was given the task of re-forming a 51st Highland Territorial Division to take the place of the one surrounded at St-Valéry. He threw himself into this task with enthusiasm, but was removed to join Wavell's staff as Deputy Chief of the General Staff at GHQ Middle East. Soon after he arrived, his old friend and mentor was replaced by Auchinleck, with results that have been described.

After his dismissal on 25 June 1942, and a brief rest in Palestine, he returned to Britain where he was sympathetically received by Churchill, and was appointed to command the 52nd (Lowland) Division, training for mountain warfare, an appointment which he found a welcome contrast, even though he reverted to the rank of Major-General. In 1944 he was promoted again to Lieutenant-General to command 12th Corps, and in that capacity fought in Dempsey's Second Army in Montgomery's 21st Army Group throughout the campaign in North-west Europe. Montgomery never gave him the glamorous jobs: always the steady, hard-slogging ones, which suited Ritchie well.

After the war he was appointed to Scottish Command, and, in 1947, as a General, he returned to his boyhood scene of Malaya as Commander-in-Chief Far East Land Forces until 1949. In 1950 he was posted to Washington as head of the British Army Staff in the Joint Services Mission to the USA, from which he retired in 1951 to Canada. There he remained for the rest of his life, taking an active part in commerce. He died on 11 December 1983.

NOTES

A number of sources are referred to in abbreviated form, as follows:

Barnett	*Desert Generals*, Correlli Barnett, Allen & Unwin 1960 and 1983.
Carver	*Tobruk*, Michael Carver, Batsford 1964
Churchill	*The Second World War*, Sir Winston S. Churchill, Cassell.
Connell	*Auchinleck*, John Connell, Cassell 1959.
Hamilton	Vol. I: *Monty. The Making of a General*, Nigel Hamilton, Hamish Hamilton 1981.
	Vol. 2: *Monty. Master of the Battlefield*, Nigel Hamilton, Hamish Hamilton 1983.
Hinsley	*British Intelligence in the Second World War: Its Influence on Strategy and Operations*, HMSO 1979, 1981.
Lewin	*The Chief*, Ronald Lewin, Hutchinson 1980.
Liddell Hart	*The Tanks*, B. H. Liddell Hart, Cassell 1959.
Playfair	*Official History of the Second World War. The Mediterranean and the Middle East*, edited by Major-General Playfair and others.
Ritchie	The Ritchie papers (see Preface)
Rommel	*The Rommel Papers*, edited by B. H. Liddell Hart, Cassell 1953.
The Sidi Rezeg Battles 1941	Official South African History, Agar-Hamilton and Turner, Oxford 1957.

Preface

1. Connell.
2. Barnett. Page numbers of 1983 edition.
3. *Memoirs*, Field Marshal Montgomery, Collins 1958.
4. A brief biography of General Ritchie is at Appendix.
5. Ritchie. Letter to Mrs Donald Brownlow, 21 May 1981.
6. Lieutenant-General Sir Alan Cunningham.
7. General (later Field Marshal) Sir John Dill.
8. Lieutenant-General W. H. E. Gott. Killed on his way to command Eighth Army on 7 August 1942.
9. Lieutenant-General (later Lord) C. W. M. Norrie.
10. Major-General F. W. (later Lieutenant-General Sir Frank) Messervy.

Chapter 1   Victory over the Italians

1. Major-General Sir Patrick Hobart.
2. Lieutenant-General (later Field Marshal Sir Henry) Maitland Wilson. GOC-in-C British Troops in Egypt. Later Commander Ninth Army and Supreme Allied Commander, Mediterranean.
3. General Sir Archibald (later Earl) Wavell.
4. Major-General M. O'Moore Creagh.
5. Lieutenant-General R. N. (later General Sir Richard) O'Connor.
6. Lieutenant-Colonel (later Major-General) J. C. Campbell. He won the VC in command of the Support Group at Sidi Rezegh in November 1941 and was killed in a car crash in February 1942, a few weeks after he had taken over command of the division.
7. Lieutenant-General (later General) Sir William Platt.
8. Quoted in Lewin, p. 82.
9. Churchill, Vol. II, p. 90.
10. ibid. p. 93.
11. Brigadier A. F. Harding (later Field Marshal Lord Harding of Petherton). Commanded 7th Armoured Division August 1942–January 1943.

Chapter 2   Back to Battleaxe

1. Lewin, p. 119.
2. Lieutenant-General P. (later Sir Philip) Neame VC.
3. Playfair, Vol. II, p. 6.
4. Major-General L. J. (later Lieutenant-General Sir Leslie) Morshead.
5. Lewin, p. 119.
6. Brigadier H. B. Latham. After the war, head of the War Office Historical Branch.
7. Lieutenant-General Sir Noel Beresford-Peirse.
8. Churchill, Vol. III, p. 302.
9. ibid. p. 304.
10. Milton, *Paradise Lost*.
11. Brigadier (later Major-General) A. H. Gatehouse. Commanded 10th Armoured Division at El Alamein.
12. Brigadier H. E. Russell, killed in September 1941 in an air crash, when BGS of 30th Corps.

Chapter 3.   Crusader

1. Churchill, Vol. III, p. 353.
2. Connell, pp. 251–2.
3. Churchill, Vol. III, p. 355.
4. Admiral Sir Andrew (later Admiral of the Fleet Viscount) Cunningham. Commander-in-Chief Mediterranean Fleet.
5. Air Marshal Sir Arthur (later Marshal of the Royal Air Force Lord) Tedder. AOC-in-C Middle East.
6. Zur besonderen Verfügung. One of its regiments, Afrika Regiment 361, was largely composed of Germans who had served in the French Foreign Legion.

7. Major-General R. M. Scobie.
8. Major-General B. C. (later Lieutenant-General Lord) Freyberg VC.
9. Brigadier H. R. B. Watkins.
10. Major-General G. L. Brink.
11. Carver, p. 38.
12. *The Sidi Rezeg Battles 1941*, pp. 61–70.
13. Brigadier G. M. O. Davy.
14. Brigadier J. Scott-Cockburn.
15. Brigadier B. F. Armstrong.
16. The British 22nd Guards Brigade, commanded by Brigadier J. C. O. Marriott, provided a third infantry brigade for 1st South African Division, which only had two of its own, 1st and 5th.
17. Brigadier D. H. Pienaar.
18. Carver, p. 73.
19. Brigadier H. E. Barrowclough.
20. Brigadier A. (later Lieutenant-General Sir Alexander) Galloway.
21. Connell, p. 365.
22. Air Vice-Marshal A. (later Air Marshal Sir Arthur) Coningham.
23. Churchill, Vol. III, p. 510.
24. Lieutenant-General Sir Arthur Smith.
25. Carver, p. 113.
26. ibid. p. 122.
27. *The Sidi Rezeg Battles*, p. 407.
28. Carver, p. 125.
29. Field Marshal Albert Kesselring, as German C-in-C South at Rome, was Rommel's immediate German superior. Marshal Ugo Cavallero, at *Comando Supremo* in Rome, was the immediate superior of General Bastico of *Supercomando Africa Settentrionale* (High Command North Africa), to whom Rommel was operationally subordinate.
30. Churchill, Vol. IV, p. 541.
31. Playfair, Vol. III, p. 435.
32. This matter is dealt with in detail in Liddell Hart, pp. 93–98 and 102; in Playfair, Vol. III, App. 8; in *The Sidi Rezeg Battles*, pp. 36–44.
33. See the very interesting extract from 'Feldzug in Afrika' in *The Sidi Rezeg Battles*, pp. 56–58.
34. Quoted in *The Sidi Rezeg Battles*, as part of a well balanced judgement on the issue, on pp. 50–51.

Chapter 4   Back to Gazala

1. Major-General H. (later Lieutenant-General Sir Herbert) Lumsden.
2. Major-General F. (later Lieutenant-General Sir Francis) Tuker.
3. Later Lieutenant-General Sir Harold Briggs, Commanded 5th Indian Division in Gazala Battles.
4. Later Major-General. Commanded 1st Armoured Division at El Alamein.
5. No. 110, quoted in full in his final despatch. App. 6. pp. 69–70.
6. Hinsley, Vol. II, p. 336.
7. Playfair, Vol. III, p. 142.

8. Ritchie, Signal OW175 of 26 January 1942.
9. Playfair, Vol. III, p. 149.
10. Connell, pp. 445–446.
11. ibid. p. 443.
12. Barrie Pitt, *The Crucible of War*, Cape 1980, p. 478.
13. Connell, p. 452.
14. Brigadier G. W. E. J. (later General Sir George) Erskine, in a letter to Brigadier Latham, Historical Section, Cabinet Office, dated 8 October 1949, of which he sent a copy to the author. He wrote: 'Gott always urged that Tobruk should only be garrisoned at all, if we were going to fight on the Gazala line in earnest. The first conception of the Gazala position was that it was an outpost on which we should delay the enemy as long as we could and then fall back to the frontier. ... The frontier was not an ideal position for defence, but it was a good deal better than Gazala, provided we had a strong armoured force to protect the southern flank.'
15. Carver, p. 164.

Chapter 5   Gazala – the first phase

1. Rommel, pp. 206–208.
2. Barnett, p. 140.
3. Connell, pp. 504–508.
4. Lieutenant-General T. W. Corbett. Dismissed at same time as Auchinleck and Dorman-Smith in August 1942. Retired 1943. An Indian Cavalry officer.
5. Public Record Office file WO 169/4033.
6. Connell, pp. 514–6.
7. WO 169/3910.
8. Connell. p. 516.
9. ibid. pp. 517–8.
10. WO 169/4033.
11. Hinsley, pp. 362–366 and Appendix 16.
12. WO 169/3936.
13. WO 169/4053.
14. Barnett, pp. 145–6.
15. WO 169/4216.
16. *Men of Valour*, Olivia Fitzroy. Quoted in Carver, p. 179.
17. Brigadier (later Major-General) J. M. L. Renton.
18. WO 169/4226.
19. WO 169/4086.
20. WO 169/4033.
21. WO 169/4053.
22. Lieutenant-Colonel H. E. (later General Sir Harold) Pyman. BGS 30th Corps and Second Army in N.W. Europe 1944–5. DCIGS 1958–61. C-in-C Allied Forces Northern Europe 1961–3.
23. WO 169/4053.
24. WO 169/4216.
25. Brigadier G. W. Richards. Later commanded 23rd Armoured Brigade and

finished the war as Major-General (Armoured Fighting Vehicles) at HQ 21st Army Group. He had been GSO1 7th Armoured Division in *Crusader*.

26. Lieutenant-Colonel G. P. B. Roberts. Later commanded 22nd and 26th Armoured Brigades in North Africa and 11th Armoured Division in N.W. Europe.
27. Carver, pp. 177–182.
28. WO 169/4033.
29. WO 169/4053.
30. WO 169/4251.
31. WO 169/3923.
32. ibid.
33. Ritchie. Signal U998.
34. ibid. Signal CS1131.
35. ibid. Signal CS1132.
36. Renumbered again from 200.
37. Rommel, p. 207.
38. WO 169/4053.
39. ibid.
40. Rommel, p. 209.
41. Connell, p. 525.
42. Rommel, p. 211.
43. WO 169/3910.
44. ibid.
45. WO 169/3936.
46. Rommel, p. 211.
47. Ritchie. Signal CS1143.
48. Brigadier J. F. M. (later General Sir John) Whiteley. Deputy Chief of Staff to General Eisenhower at Allied Force HQ Algiers and at SHAEF in N.W. Europe 1943–5; DCIGS 1948–51.
49. Ritchie was ill-informed by his GSO1(SD), Lieut-Colonel Belchem. First Armoured Brigade included both 1st and 6th Royal Tanks, who had been in Egypt before the war and had been involved in operations in 1940 and 1941. They were exceptionally 'desertworthy'.
50. Ritchie.
51. WO 169/4145.
52. WO 169/3910.
53. Ritchie.

Chapter 6   The Cauldron

1. Major-General W. H. C. Ramsden. Commanded 30th Corps July–September 1942.
2. Connell, p. 533.
3. Carver, pp. 250–262.
4. Brigadier F. W. (later Major-General Sir Francis) de Guingand. Chief of Staff HQ Eighth Army 1942–3. Chief of Staff 21st Army Group N.W. Europe 1944–5.
5. Connell, p. 533.

6. Agar-Hamilton and Turner, *Crisis in the Desert*, Oxford 1952, p. 73.
7. Ritchie. Letter DO/70/6 of 3 June 1942.
8. Ritchie. Signal CS1186.
9. WO 169/3924.
10. Rommel, pp. 549–50.
11. Lieutenant-Colonel (later Major-General) R. F. K. Belchem. BGS (Ops) HQ 21st Army Group 1944–5.
12. Carver, p. 212.
13. 30th Corps War Diary 9 June. WO 169/4033.
14. WO 169/4086.
15. WO 169/4033.
16. WO 169/4086.
17. ibid.
18. WO 169/4033.
19. WO 169/3936.
20. Playfair, Vol. III, p. 241.
21. Lieutenant-Colonel (later Major-General) H. R. B. Foote VC.

Chapter 7   The Fall of Tobruk

1. Playfair, Vol. III, p. 197.
2. Connell, p. 565. The original is in Ritchie's papers.
3. Churchill, vol. IV, p. 331.
4. Connell, p. 565.
5. *Crisis in the Desert*, p. 73.
6. Signal 0/11580, quoted by Connell, p. 566. Ritchie's copy uses the word 'ready' for 'able', a difference due, no doubt, to decipherment. Time of origin was 0915 GMT, which was 1215 local, not 1115, as given by Connell.
7. Signal 0/11603, quoted by Connell, p. 566.
8. Ritchie.
9. Playfair, Vol. III, p. 246.
10. Hinsley, p. 384.
11. Rommel, p. 223.
12. Playfair, Vol. III, p. 246.
13. Signal CS1257, quoted by Connell, p. 567.
14. Signal U1405, quoted by Playfair, Vol. III, p. 248 and Connell, p. 568.
15. Ritchie. ADC's diary.
16. Connell, p. 572.
17. Churchill, Vol. IV, p. 328.
18. Connell, p. 572.
19. Ritchie.
20. *Crisis in the Desert*, p. 102.
21. Connell, p. 574.
22. Ritchie. Signal U1425. Connell, p. 573.
23. Connell, p. 575.
24. WO 169/3924.
25. *Crisis in the Desert*, p. 101.
26. Connell, p. 576.

27. ibid.
28. ibid. pp. 577–8.
29. Major-General H. B. Klopper.
30. Connell, p. 578.
31. ibid. p. 579.
32. WO 169/4216.
33. Brigadier D. W. Reid.
34. *Crisis in the Desert*, p. 120.
35. Ritchie. Connell, p. 583.
36. WO 169/3910.
37. ibid.
38. WO 169/4216.
39. Liddell Hart, *The Tanks* II, p. 183.
40. Connell, p. 583.
41. Ritchie. Signal U1563.
42. Connell, p. 587.
43. Playfair, Vol. III p. 259.
44. *Crisis in the Desert*, p. 157.
45. Brigadier A. C. Willison.
46. *Crisis in the Desert*, p. 129.
47. Ritchie. Signal U1618, quoted by Connell, p. 589.
48. WO 169/3936.
49. Brigadier A. Anderson.
50. Connell, pp. 589–90.
51. Later Lieutenant-General Sir Ian Freeland. GOC Northern Ireland 1968–71.
52. Ritchie. Signal U1635.
53. ibid. Signal CS1299.
54. WO 169/3924.
55. *Crisis in the Desert*, pp. 208–210.
56. Petrol, oil and lubricants.
57. *Crisis in the Desert*, pp. 208–210.
58. ibid, p. 203, Note 2.
59. On 19 June Renton had relieved Messervy in command of 7th Armoured Division, the latter having been dismissed as a result of his failure to support 29th and 20th Indian brigades.
60. WO 169/4080.
61. *Crisis in the Desert*, map p. 204.
62. WO 169/4216.
63. Ritchie. Signal R3.
64. *Crisis in the Desert*, p. 235.
65. Connell, p. 596.
66. Major-General T. W. Rees.
67. Lieutenant-General W. G. Holmes.
68. *Crisis in the Desert*, p. 235.
69. Playfair, Vol. III, p. 281.
70. *Crisis in the Desert*, p. 236.
71. Ritchie. Signal CS 1314.

72. *Crisis in the Desert*, p. 235.
73. Connell, p. 612.
74. Playfair, Vol. III, pp. 286–7.

Chapter 8   First and Second Alamein

1. Playfair, Vol. III, p. 294.
2. Hinsley, p. 402 *et seq.*
3. Playfair, Vol. III, p. 334.
4. ibid. p. 353. Hinsley, p. 405, gives different figures: 21st Panzer 10 fit tanks on 17 July and 15th Panzer 13 on 19 July, quoting WO 201/2154 No. 263 of 18 and No. 264 of 19 July 1942.
5. Hinsley, p. 405.
6. Brigadier G. H. Clifton. He was captured, but escaped, dressed as a private soldier. He was captured again in the Battle of Alam Halfa, escaped, but was recaptured. See also my *Tobruk*, p. 89, and *El Alamein*, p. 71.
7. Connell, p. 691.
8. Churchill, Vol. IV, p. 465.
9. Montgomery, p. 94.
10. Connell, p. 716.
11. Barnett, pp. 259–262.
12. ibid. pp. 200–201.
13. Hamilton, Vol. 1, pp. 500–632.
14. Carver, p. 197.
15. ibid. pp. 200–201.
16. Hamilton, Vol. II, pp. 11–28.
17. Brigadier F. E. W. (later General Sir Frank) Simpson.
18. ibid. p. 68.

Chapter 9   Wash-Up

1. General Sir David Fraser, *And We Shall Shock Them*, Hodder & Stoughton 1983, pp. 224–7.
2. Carver, p. 260.
3. Hamilton, Vol. I, p. 732 *et seq.*
4. Carver, p. 254.
5. ibid. pp. 253–4.

INDEX

Officers are described by the highest rank they held during the period.